WRESTLING WITH
GOD

WRESTLING WITH
GOD

STORIES OF DOUBT
AND FAITH

BARBARA FALCONER NEWHALL

Patheos Press
4700 South Syracuse Street, Suite 400
Denver, Colorado 80237
Patheos.com

Cover design by Michelle Lenger

Newhall, Barbara Falconer.
Wrestling With God: Stories of Doubt and Faith / Barbara Falconer Newhall
ISBN: 978-1-939221-25-4 (paperback)

For my father and mother, Dave and Tinka Falconer,
who lived with the questions

Apprehend God in all things, for God is in all things.
Every single creature is full of God, and is a book
about God.
~ *Meister Eckhart*, 1260–1328

Faith and doubt aren't opposites.
Doubt is often a sign that your faith has a pulse.
~ *Rob Bell*

CONTENTS

FOREWORD

Barbara Falconer Newhall has spent a lot of time, as I have, writing about religion for a daily newspaper. We were working back in the days before journalism professors began referring to these now-antiquated ink-and-paper publications as "legacy media." Those of us on the God beat had one of the more difficult—and in our eyes interesting—jobs on the newspaper. We wrote about faith while sticking to the facts.

Secular journalists and people of faith were on the front lines of the culture wars. At the same time, we lived in different worlds. Journalists sought out stories with drama and conflict and spiritual hypocrisy, themes that were never too hard to find on the religion beat. But the people we were writing about—people of faith—were more into the business of reconciliation.

As reporters for daily newspapers, we covered breaking news, while religionists sought out timeless truth. The more intelligent people of faith we came across were engaged in nuanced theological debate, while our editors favored sound bites and a snappy lead paragraph.

We were skeptics. They were believers.

What I love about this book is how Barbara Newhall, with

honesty and grace, bridges those two worlds. She tells her own story—something we were *not* encouraged to do back in the old days—but she does not let that get in the way of chronicling the spiritual journeys of the people she profiles in these pages.

Newhall goes out of her way to include people of all traditions—and no tradition—in this work. There are atheists, activists, contemplatives, thinkers, and people who lean toward pious devotion. She has tried to bring these people to us as they really are, to capture their voice and spirit. And she has succeeded.

We cannot really be "objective" when writing about religion, but we can be fair and respectful of other peoples' beliefs. In *Wrestling with God*, Newhall does exactly that. And it's a refreshing perspective amidst the "new atheism" of snarky commentators like the late Christopher Hitchens or Bill Maher, the otherwise smart talk show host who gets stunningly simple-minded when the subject shifts from politics to religion. True believers—whether they are in the "New Age," evangelical Christian, or Islamist movements—are easy to parody, but we do so at the risk of our own understanding.

If you believe what you see on TV or the World Wide Web, modern civilization is under attack by forces of narrow-minded, intolerant religious fundamentalists—all the way from Fallujah to Florida. The real story, at least in the United States, is less alarming and more interesting. We are not really falling into fundamentalism, nor are we finally coming to our senses and embracing a new atheism.

We are, in fact, wrestling with God.

Statistics, especially religion statistics, are notoriously easy to manipulate, but with that proviso allow me to include a few paragraphs full of numbers.

A recent Pew survey asked Americans whether they agreed

with the statement "many religions can lead to eternal life." Seventy percent of people affiliated with a religion or denomination said they did. Even a surprising 57 percent of "evangelical Christians" said there is more than one way to heaven.

Meanwhile, Gallup pollsters asked, "Do you think of spirituality more in a personal and individual sense or more in terms of organized religion and church doctrine?" Almost three-quarters said "personal and individual." Similarly, one-third of the Americans surveyed by Gallup now call themselves "spiritual but not religious."

Most of these people are not atheists; nine out of ten Americans believe in God. But what kind of God? Another survey found that more than eight of ten Americans saw God as "everywhere and in everything," as opposed to "someone somewhere." The old anthropomorphic deity is giving way to the more abstract impersonal force, as in "may the Force be with you."

Barbara Newhall and I grew up in the 1950s, when not going to church was believed to be a stepping-stone to communism. But there has since been an incredible shift in attitudes in the U.S. about church attendance and religious tradition. In 1958, *only one in twenty-five* Americans said he or she had left the religion or religious denomination of his or her childhood. By 1984, *one out of three* of us had switched religions or religious denominations.

So, yes, we *are* wrestling with God.

Between our rounds of divine wrestling, it might be a good idea for us to step back and start talking to one another about God. Barbara told me that her idea for this project was to put representatives of various wisdom traditions together in a book so they could "talk" to each other, like next door neighbors talking over the back fence.

The conversation will probably lead to less confrontation and more reconciliation. In fact, that process has already begun. Barbara recounted a story about a progressive-minded friend of hers who asked her how she—as the liberal author—felt about the more conservative people she interviewed for her book. Without thinking, Barbara blurted out "I'm like God. I love them all!"

Newhall went into this project not just intent upon telling a good story. She wanted to write a book that would inspire and help people of every faith tradition. And she thought these stories would be especially enlightening to all the doubters, skeptics, and seekers in the fastest growing religion in America, those folks who belong to "none of the above," yet are still keeping an open mind.

One of those was the author herself. In putting together this book, Barbara was on her own kind of spiritual search. She was looking for a new way to believe in God in a globalized, secularized, multi-faith, 21st-century world that worships the scientific method. Perhaps all this conversation would lead to some kind of divine revelation. Perhaps she would finally see the light.

In the end, there were no thunderbolts. There was, however, a subtle yet powerful shift. "With the help of my interviewees," she told me, "I did arrive at a place that to my surprise I have to call 'faith.'"

My suggestion to those holding this book in their hands is to simply read it with the same kind of open mind and an open heart and see where it leads.

—Don Lattin, San Francisco

Don Lattin (www.donlattin.com) covered the religion beat at the San Francisco Chronicle *for more than two decades. He is the author of five books on American religion and spirituality, the most recent of which is titled* Distilled Spirits.

PART ONE: *Wrestling With God*

1

Losing God

"What I don't understand, Barbara, is why a smart, attractive woman like you would want to believe in God. To me, religion is irrational. It's an emotional crutch," the woman sitting across from me was saying. She was everything I wanted to be—intelligent and successful, with interesting friends and a couple of books to her credit. Even her hair was perfectly coiffed, blond and orderly, and her clothes, though casual, looked as though they'd come from a department store I couldn't afford.

I was at a writers' conference in Squaw Valley, high in the Sierra Nevada. During the winter this place was a famous ski resort. But it was summer now, and we were sitting in the ski lodge cafeteria at a metal table built to withstand spilt coffee and the clank of ski boots. The woman across from me was one of the presenters at the conference, and she was generously giving me a half hour of feedback on the beginnings of a book—this one— about my search for God in the lives and spiritual struggles of ordinary people.

Suddenly, mid-conversation, my mentor interrupted herself and leaned across the table to ask me why I would want to believe in God. "I can see why people living in squalor and ignorance would need the comfort of religion," she said. "But why would you?"

Why indeed? It's a question I'd been asking myself for most of my adult life. At the time of this conversation, I had been a practicing Christian on and off—with lots of off—for years. And though my attendance on Sunday mornings was spotty, I belonged to a church. Did I actually believe in God? Not really. Yet deep down I felt something was missing from my life, something big. So I'd show up in church from time to time hoping that God, too, would show up in some tangible, concrete way, bringing reassurance that, yes, a loving, intentional force was at work in the universe, and that, yes, I mattered. Every now and then, at church or elsewhere, I'd get a fleeting glimpse of something that might have been the God I was looking for. But most of the time God was a no-show.

Which is why I wrote this book—to see if I could get God to show up. Did it happen? Yes, but not in the way I expected. Did I move from doubt to faith? Yes, but I went there kicking and screaming. The word "faith" can be a troublesome one for me. In some contexts it has a cloying, self-satisfied feel to it. But if I look at faith from another angle, if faith means trust, then yes, at the end of my journey I did wind up with something I had to concede was faith. Faith that nothing was missing from my life. Faith that everything was, and always had been, right there in front of me.

When I was a child, God was very real to me. As a little kid in Detroit I loved Sunday school at our local Presbyterian church, and later as a teenager I looked forward to choir practice and youth group. The others in my family were indifferent churchgoers: My father was a lapsed Methodist. My mother had been Catholic as a girl, but undertook an extended leave of absence from her church when she married my father. My brothers—well, they just didn't find God all that interesting.

But I did. I believed in God, and I loved Jesus, the Galilean carpenter who walked on water and calmed the raging sea, who gave sight to the blind, who cared for the poor and the weak as well as the powerful, who died and rose from the dead, as I would someday. God was real to me in those long-ago days. God's existence was not something I arrived at intellectually. It was something I just knew.

One summer day when I was twelve years old, I fell asleep on a beach and got a glimpse of God face-to-face. The encounter, God's and mine, took place near my family's summer cottage at the spot where a small, murky-brown channel—alive with minnows, polliwogs, algae, decaying weeds, bits of oak leaf, and rotting birch bark—empties itself into the great, blue Lake Michigan.

I was flat on my back. The sun was warm, and a touch of air was moving in off the lake. I fell into sleep, and there awaiting me, of course, was God. Around me, below me, above me was God. God knows who I am, I thought. Of course he does. How could it be otherwise? I turned as warm and liquid as the water flowing past me into the lake.

All too soon, something woke me up—the sun going behind a cloud, a seagull snapping its wings overhead—and I drifted up from sleep. I was back on my beach. God, the vividness, the clarity of it, was gone, but I felt embraced by the world as it truly was.

Things changed when I graduated from high school and went off to Ann Arbor and the University of Michigan. I told my first academic advisor that I liked to read, and he signed me up for a course in Great Books. Eagerly I dove into Lucretius, Aristotle, Virgil, Dante, Milton. My freshman year, instead of God, I thought about books.

For my sophomore Philosophy 101 class, I acquired a fat red book of eight hundred plus pages. It was *Being and Nothingness,* by Jean-Paul Sartre. I thought Sartre was awfully long-winded, but my philosophy professor seemed to think he spoke the truth. Our lives have no meaning, Sartre claimed. That's the Nothingness. The Being is—we go ahead and live them anyway. We make do without God, we tough it out.

Later we read Bertrand Russell, who took great pleasure in unleashing his wit upon Christianity and its adherents. Religion is based on fear, he wrote, "partly the terror of the unknown and partly . . . the wish to feel that you have a kind of elder brother who will stand by you in all your troubles." We must learn to stand on our own two feet, Russell admonished; we must get along without God.

I was unable to stand on my own two feet against Russell, Sartre, and my philosophy professor. I decided that if I wanted to be taken seriously in academia and in the professional world beyond, if I wanted to think of myself as an intellectual, I'd probably have to do without God.

This was a sad realization, frightening even. I was facing a world without meaning in which I was an inconsequential accident of atoms and space. There was no God up there looking out for me and throwing good things my way. I realized with a thud that finding a life partner, getting a career started, and making the big moral choices would be up to me from now on. I'd be on my own. I'd have to tough it out.

In zoology class, our frogs had to be pithed before we could dissect them. To pith a frog you hold the squirming creature in your hand and press a pick along the top of its skull, into its brain. Now your frog is dead and you can cut open its belly. Some of my lab mates didn't want to pith their frogs. They were squeamish, but I wasn't. I was tough and proud of it. I showed off. I pithed their frogs for them.

By the time I graduated from Michigan, I had concluded that Russell was right. Sartre was right. Darwin, Nietzsche, Freud, and Marx were right. Pith the frog. Cut it open. Inside you'll see that its innards look a lot like human innards. What you see is what you get; there is no meaning beyond that; live with it.

And that is what I have done for much of my life—tough it out. Every once in a while, I'll find myself on that Lake Michigan beach, or I'll be writing something, or taking a photograph, or talking with a fellow traveler on the journey, and I'll feel God's presence. And for a breathless moment, I'll remember and think, yes, God is here. Of course God is here. How could it be otherwise? But that is only some of the time. Most of the time, I have lived with the otherwise.

2

On the Religion Beat

My questioner at that Squaw Valley writers' conference was a successful, hardheaded journalist, and I didn't want her to write me off as a sentimental puffball, so I dodged her questions. How could I admit to her that what she dismissed as an emotional crutch—God—was the very thing I longed for?

But making my way unscathed through her skepticism wasn't the real problem here. I too was a skeptical, hardheaded journalist. In the years since my student days at the University of Michigan, secularism, pop culture, the sexual revolution, and multiculturalism—*post-modernity*—had pretty much finished the job that Sartre and Russell, science, biblical criticism, and the privileging of empirical evidence—*modernity*—had begun back in Ann Arbor.

Nonetheless, a few years before that meeting in the mountains, I had worked up the courage to act upon my yearnings in spite of myself, to investigate them. I had reasoned that, just because I couldn't smell, taste, or see God, or use the road map of logic to arrive at God's doorstep did not mean that there was no such thing. And if there was a divine something somewhere in the universe, a creative, intentional, benevolent force—out there or right here, or both—I wanted a piece of it. If there was a party going on, I wanted to be in on it. I'd put aside the perturbations of Bertrand Russell and Jean-Paul Sartre and go looking for the sacred, for the divine, for what I as a Westerner had grown up calling God.

But how do I track down this elusive entity, this absentee, and most likely non-existent deity? How do I wrestle it back into my life? Do I read up on ancient scripture? Go on a pilgrimage to Lourdes? To Bodh Gaya? Take an adult ed class at the city rec department? Google it?

Usually, when I need to locate something—a reliable periodontist or a deer-proof ground cover for the back yard—I ask somebody. I go with the common sense of people I respect. As a journalist, I was used to asking questions. I had put in my time at places like *Good Housekeeping* magazine, the *San Francisco Chronicle*, and the *Oakland Tribune*. Over the years, I had asked strangers the most personal of questions—about their marital problems, their drug addictions, the disposition of their mortal remains, whether they'd been circumcised and what did they think of that? I'd done whatever I had to do to get the story. Ride into town on the itchy, bristly back of an elephant to write the circus story. Jump into the water with a 1,400-pound whale to interview the guy who cleaned its tank.

So, when a religion reporting job came up at the *Contra Costa Times* in Walnut Creek, not far from my home on the eastern shore of San Francisco Bay, I grabbed it. Maybe, I thought, I can get my questions answered on the religion beat. Maybe, just maybe, that's where I'll be able to wrestle this slippery God of mine back into my life.

I met believers of every stripe on the religion beat: A Zoroastrian priest. A Catholic who said she was having daily appari-

tions of the Virgin Mary. A twelve-year-old boy who had vowed
to remain celibate until marriage. An intelligence analyst at the
Lawrence Livermore Lab who thought the world was going to end
next Monday, Tuesday at the latest.

As fascinating as religion reporting was, it frustrated me. Typically, I'd have one hour max to do an interview about the new
stained glass windows or the vacation Bible school before I had to
rush back to the paper to meet my deadline. There was no time to
ask the intimate questions that mattered most to me. Questions
like, what is God like? How do you know? Where does God show
up in your life? What difference does that presence make?

Four years into my stint on the religion beat, tendonitis in my
arms and wrists brought my decades-long newspaper career to a
halt. It was a painful transition for me. I missed the excitement
of the city room and the companionship of my newspaper colleagues. I especially missed all those intriguing religion beat conversations. But now, with extra time at my disposal, I realized that
something new was opening up to me. I had time to go back and
finish some of those conversations. I could start new ones.

Eventually, a plan took shape. I would go back into the field.
I'd interview a cross-section of people in all their spiritual diversity and distinctiveness—the same kinds of people I'd met on the
religion beat at the *Contra Costa Times*. But this time I would
take my time. I'd do the interviews in depth and write a book.
I would seek out thoughtful, successful people in my area, and
I'd ask them the tough questions, including the one my journalist
colleague was to ask me so bluntly, "Why would a smart, attractive person like you want to believe in God?" With any luck at all,
their answers would open up a window on the God who'd gone
missing from my life—for me, for my skeptical friends and newspaper colleagues, as well as for believers everywhere struggling to

hang on to their faith in a globalized, secularized, multi-cultural, twenty-first-century world that privileges the scientific method.

I started making appointments—with priests and rabbis and other clergy, but mostly with regular people who could speak from the trenches of faith. I met with people in restaurants, in offices, at their kitchen tables, on lawn chairs under the open sky. Often the interviews went on for hours. By the time I was done, I'd had heart-to-hearts about God with Christians, Jews, Muslims, Hindus, Buddhists, Native Americans, a Witch, and even an atheist or two. To my surprise, I found that most of the people I talked to were facing my same dilemma—the challenge of reconciling the irrefutable findings of science and modernity with a life of the spirit. Like so many Westerners, they faced a stubborn conflict between mind and soul, reason and passion. And their various responses fascinated me.

Meanwhile, as I talked about this book with friends, certain questions came up again and again: What did all those people I was talking to have in common, my friends wanted to know. What universal truths ran through the various religions? What is God like, *really*? I sensed a poignancy to their questions. My friends seemed to be saying, "What can I believe? And, how can my beliefs be true if all those other beliefs are also true?

Seyyed Hossein Nasr, an Iranian-born professor of Islamic studies at George Washington University, has given a lot of thought to those questions, to the apparent irreconcilability of the world's religious traditions—and to the fact that each tradition claims to have a handle on the truth.

"Every religion has a form," he says. "And yet no two religions have the same form, though there are similarities. But there is only one Center. There is only one Ultimate Reality. The lines of all religions converge at only one point."

To speak of the sacred is to speak of the Formless, Nasr says. The Formless penetrates the world through such forms as the Christian Eucharist and *salah*, the daily prayers of Islam. There is no need to be confounded by the differences—"Religious divergence is itself the will of Heaven."

Walt Whitman expressed this point of view nicely in his 1855 poem "Song of Myself"

> *Do I contradict myself?*
> *Very well then I contradict myself,*
> *(I am large, I contain multitudes.)*

The people in this book, as varied and distinctive as they are, have this in common: Like me, they are looking for meaning, for that ultimate reality. They are aware of their yearnings, they respect them and they act upon them. Surrounded as they are by the challenges of modern secular life, they have the courage and imagination to follow their deepest desires. They have a sense of adventure. They have opened their eyes to God—as Brahman, as Nirvana, as the *mysterium tremendum*, as the ground of being, as the wonder of a fourteen-billion-year-old, unfolding universe that, miraculously, includes them. They are asking questions of the universe and insisting on answers. They are wrestling with God.

And so, if the spirit that finds expression through the voices on these pages seems fraught with contradiction, so be it. Maybe that tells us something about the deepest reality. *It is large. It is everywhere. It contains multitudes.*

PART TWO: *Religion vs. Science*

3

The Happy Atheist

The story of my search for God begins with an atheist named Anthony Mack. Anthony happens to be one of the first people I interviewed for this project, but his story is also the best place to begin because it is the starting place for my own journey—that rational, skeptical place that asserts that if you can't prove God's existence you must therefore live as if there is no God. It's the place I kept getting stuck in on and off throughout my adult life.

Ironically, that early interviewee, atheist though he was and is, gave me an important clue as to where my spiritual journey might end, and that is—with joy. Anthony is one of the most delightful, that is to say one of the most delight-filled, people I know. He calls himself a "happy atheist." Unlike author-atheists Christopher Hitchens (*God Is Not Great*), Richard Dawkins (*The God Delusion*), and Sam Harris (*Letter to a Christian Nation*), Anthony is not as much interested in finding fault with religion as he is in declaring his passion for the world as it is.

"I don't need religion to have a profound sense of the wonder and magic and mystery of the universe," he told me during our first conversation. "I love the whole miraculous evolutionary process. Three-and-a-half-billion years of ever-increasing complexity and mind-blowing diversity. Lichen, jellyfish, dinosaurs, human beings. The scientific world view gives me that. It lets me understand and relish the universe as it actually is."

A senior software engineer, Anthony lives with his wife and daughter in the Southern California town of Silverado, at the end of a long, one-lane dirt road that winds across a creek to a high hillside overlooking Ladd Canyon and a generous slice of the natural world.

Anthony grew up in Laguna Beach, California. His mother and father were both born in England and reared in the Church of England. His mother left Christianity for the Self-Realization Fellowship, a Los Angeles-based religious organization with origins in Kriya Yoga. His father rejected the Church of England and religion entirely. The young Anthony, as a result, witnessed frequent family discussions about the existence of God. Because of his mother, he was a fervent believer as a boy. When he was about fourteen years old, however, Anthony realized that he wasn't a little kid anymore and he began to wonder—was God just a myth? It was time to find out.

Anthony's story begins with a youthful experiment in metaphysics.

Anthony Mack—His Story

I was on a search for God. I was a teenager, fourteen, maybe fifteen years old, and I wanted to know, did God really exist—or not? I was having my doubts. I had been a believer up to that point, but I was getting smarter and smarter, and God was looking more and more like a myth to me.

It seemed to me that if everything I'd been taught was true, and God really could hear prayers, and God really was powerful and could do miracles, and God really did care about me and wanted me to choose him—if all this was true, then of course God would want to give me enough information, enough *evidence*, to know that he was there so I could start looking for him and find him and choose him.

And so one night, as I was sitting alone at the dinner table—my dinner plate had peas on it and probably something like mashed potatoes and a pork chop—it occurred to me that I could do an experiment and get some answers

So I said to God, "Dear God, I'm a lost soul who wants to believe in you, and I want to feel your love, but at the same time I want to use this reasoning brain that you've graciously given me. However, when I use reason, I find that I can't believe in things without evidence. I need some evidence that you are actually there. I'm not looking for some big miracle where you appear in front of me and explain it all. I need just the minimum, a single bit, just one tiny yes or one tiny no."

Then I looked real hard at one of the peas on my plate and I said, "God, could you hover this pea for me right now? If you do, then I'll know you're there and you want me to search for you."

The pea was small and light. If God lifted it only a single inch, that would be enough. I'd see it. And I'd know that it was not a magic trick, because with a magic trick it's the magician who comes to you and says, "I'm going to make this pea or this rabbit or this elephant hover." In this case, I had picked the object myself, so if it did hover, there could be no mistake about it: a supernatural force was being applied to this pea, and God wanted me to search for him.

I was dead serious about this. I was only fourteen, fifteen years old and I really thought I was talking to God. I'd read about miracles in the Bible, and to me this one seemed so trivial. I wasn't asking God to divide the Red Sea or raise someone from the dead. I was asking for a micro-miracle that involved only a single pea rising in the air for a few seconds. And if the truth be told, I was half expecting that little pea to rise up off my dinner plate.

Well, the pea didn't hover. I tried wording my question in different ways. I tried saying it out loud. Nothing happened. That pea just sat there.

I stared at it and thought—does God not want me to choose him and be with him? Does he not hear my prayers? Where have I gone wrong? There was a lot at stake here, you see. I was planning the rest of my life around this experiment. If God said yes and the pea hovered, I'd know that I should devote my life to searching for him. If the pea didn't hover, well, then . . .

So, I said to God, "Look, if you're really as outside of time and as omniscient as everyone says you are, you know right now that the rest of my life depends on what happens here tonight. If you're listening, and you want me to look for you, here's your chance to talk to me."

Again, nothing happened. I tried a few more times and finally I said, "Okay, I give up." And I did.

I was a teenager then. I'm in my forties now. I've never gone back. It's clear that God does not want me to look for him, and I haven't, though I've given him several more chances to communicate with me over the years. Every once in a while I'll say, "Okay, let's try it again," and I'll ask God to hover a pea or some other simple thing. But as I get older and older and I get more and more sure of God's inexistence, I feel sillier and sillier asking the same old question. The more I pray to God, the more I feel like I'm talking to Zeus. My prayers feel disingenuous, so I've stopped.

But, you know, if I ever get to the Pearly Gates and God says, "Why didn't you choose me?" I'll say, "Because you never hovered that damned pea."

And that's the story of my search for God. Now, when someone asks me what religion I am, I say atheist because people are familiar with that term. But that's like saying I'm a "non-astrologist," which totally misses the point. The point is that I do, in fact, believe in something, the same thing I believed in as a teenager: I believe in the scientific method; I believe in evidence.

The scientific method is a self-correcting thought process that hasn't changed substantially since Thales of Miletus first got a fix on it twenty-six-hundred years ago. You come up with a hypothesis that attempts to explain something; you test the hypothesis by experiment, observation, or whatever might disprove it; and then you correct it as necessary. If even one experiment contradicts your hypothesis, you have to throw it out. So it's not science, or the body of knowledge produced by science, that I believe in. It's the *method* by which that knowledge is gained that I so dearly cherish.

The scientific method has taught us some amazing things about ourselves, things that thousands of years of religion have not conceived of. For example, did you know that we share an ancestor with yeast? How do we know that? Because scientists have discovered that human beings and yeast use the same cell division gene. That one gene is more than a billion years old, and it hasn't changed a bit in all that time. Isn't that neat?

I look at a rose and I see the same beauty everyone else sees—and more, because as a scientist I can see deep down into the genetic structure of the rose. I see the beauty there and I enjoy it the same way some people enjoy listening to Mozart or eating chocolate ice cream. I hate it when people tell me that I think that the material world is "all there is." Thinking that the universe is "all there is" is like thinking the Mona Lisa is just a bunch of paint.

I love life and I love every living thing, especially the complex living things that the evolutionary process has produced. I'll admit that it doesn't bother me much to kill an ant or a spider or some other arthropod if it's crawling across my kitchen sink. But a mouse? A mouse is a mammal. He looks at me. I look at him. I understand his fear. To kill a mouse hurts me. And an ape? An ape is practically human. I couldn't harm a mountain gorilla for the life of me. As for other human beings, I love them more than I can say.

I am a good person. I volunteer for the fire department. I stop at the side of the road to help stranded motorists, which is an inherently dangerous thing to do. But I do it anyway. I'm willing to take risks in order to help people. I am good, not out of fear of divine retribution, but because my parents were good people, as were their parents. The root of this behavior is in thousands of years of natural selection, of living in groups where being "good" is advantageous.

I'm a real Christmas fan. I love the Christmas tree. I love giving presents. I love decorating and hanging the stockings. I love being with my family and friends and all the good cheer. And yet, I don't believe in Jesus. As a small lad growing up in Southern California, I'd hear my mom say, "Okay, guys. Let's not forget the true meaning of Christmas." It's taken me most of my life to realize that the true meaning of Christmas isn't the birth of Jesus. It's a celebration. It's a vessel that lets people show their good will. It's about us. It's us helping each other. It's us giving to each other. It's us loving us. That's what I feel, that's what I believe.

4

A Modern-Day Burning Bush

Anthony believes in the scientific method. For him, rational knowledge alone is trustworthy and worth believing in. The trouble for Anthony, and for me, lies in that word *believe*.

Some time after I interviewed Anthony, I had a chance to hear a sermon by Marcus J. Borg, a biblical and Jesus scholar and the author of the best-selling *Meeting Jesus Again for the First Time*. Borg was preaching to the congregation of St. Giles Parish in Moraga, just over the hill from my house. The setting was a traditional chapel, where the ceilings were arched, the pews wooden, and the organ full-throated. The sermon, on the other hand, was anything but traditional. You don't have to believe, Borg told the St. Giles congregation. You don't have to believe to be a Christian.

Believe. It is a word that most Christians—most Westerners— assume is at the heart of any religious faith. If you're a Christian, for example, and you can't say all those creeds with certainty, or you're not sure about the virgin birth or, heaven forbid, the resurrection of the body, how in the world can you be a bona fide Christian? The problem lies in that word belief, Borg said. As we use it today, it is a truly modern concept, a response to the intellectual pressures of an era that prizes reason and empirical knowledge and compels the faithful to articulate their experience of God as doctrine, rather than as a relationship with a Holy One that is beyond both words and creeds.

The religious life, I learned from Borg, is not about asserting the truths of a traditional religious doctrine with the same ease and certainty that a modern person might assert the laws of gravity or the wisdom of the United States Constitution. It is about being open to God's very real presence in the world. For Borg, as a Christian, "it is about living in the Christian community, living within this tradition, letting it function as a sacrament, letting it shape our life with God."

That we humans are here at all to be aware of "the sheer wonder of Is-ness" is extraordinary, Borg said. But "actually, the truly extraordinary thing is that the world could ever look ordinary to us."

As a religion reporter at the *Contra Costa Times* I found out that, unlike Anthony, not every scientist limits what he or she knows or believes or trusts to what can be proved according to the scientific method. Like Borg, some scientists embrace the idea that there is more to existence than meets the eye. For them, God can be very much present in human life and human history. Nobel laureate Charles H. Townes is one such person.

A professor emeritus of physics at the University of California, Berkeley and the author of *How the Laser Happened: Adventures of a Scientist* and *Making Waves*, Townes was awarded the 1964 Nobel Prize in Physics for his role in the development of the laser and its precursor the maser. He describes his sudden insight into the principles underlying maser technology as a revelation from God "as luminous as Moses' burning bush."

Born in South Carolina to a Southern Baptist family, Townes has been sturdily Christian all his life. At various times he's been an Episcopalian, a Methodist, and a Presbyterian—attending whatever nearby church he and his wife thought best for themselves and their children. "Right now," he told me, "I'm a Congregationalist."

One winter evening, Townes took time out from his work to sit with me in the living room of his home high in the Berkeley hills and talk about the convergence of religion and science in theory and in his own life. He spoke without haste, his Southern origins lingering in his voice. As always, I recorded the conversation and delivered the tapes to my faithful transcriber, Marcy McGaugh. A few days later, at home in my writing room, I spread Marcy's massive typed transcription out on my desk. It was daunting.

Like so many of the highly educated people I interviewed for this book, Charles Townes was an abstract thinker, not given to wowing his listeners with juicy true-life anecdotes that short-circuit the intellect and go straight to the gut. In the hour and a half or so we had talked, the Nobel Laureate had drawn upon centuries of Western thought—abstract ideas—on the subjects of science and religion. Exactly what I needed.

At this point in my search for God, it was my intellect—my need for certainty, for what I thought of as intellectual integrity, my need to believe in God in the same way I believed in gravity—that had to be addressed, assuaged, and switched off, so that my gut could do what it needed to do, and my search for God could proceed unimpeded by my long-time, nay saying companions, Russell, Sartre, Freud, and Nietzsche.

Charles Townes was just the man for the job. He had given the subject of science and religion a lot of thought. Patiently, I sorted through the pages on my desk and listened again to what he had to say. Greedily, I dug out and highlighted what I needed to hear.

Charles H. Townes—His Story

Some people who are religious feel their faith means they have to be absolutely sure about everything. I don't take that position, yet I feel I'm religious and have great trust. I'm not sure of anything, including scientific laws. I expect the sun will rise tomorrow morning, but if somebody asked me, can you prove that it will? Well, I can't.

I don't think one can prove or disprove God's presence. I would say we have to observe—observe life, observe how people behave, observe our own feelings—and make judgments on that basis. History, civilization, families, the Bible, those are all part of the basis for our judgment as to what we think is right.

Mathematicians, a few decades ago, showed that to prove things mathematically, you must first make a set of assumptions. You can never be sure the assumptions are consistent with each other, and yet you make them. This is known as Gödel's law. With that, I'd say you can't prove anything in an absolute sense. All you can say is—well, I think it's right and I have a certain logic about it. But that doesn't mean you can't make assumptions and live by them. You may have great faith in your assumptions. More and more scientists are recognizing this. It opens up more tolerance of religion, because—just because you can't prove it, doesn't mean it's not right. You have to make a judgment.

Some people feel they have to choose between religious faith and science because of the inconsistencies between certain religious beliefs and certain scientific beliefs. For example, according to the Bible, the earth is 4,000 years or so old, and scientists know that it's much older than that. But we can find inconsistencies within scientific beliefs also. For example, gravity we believe in. We can test it. Quantum mechanics we believe in. We test it. But we can't make a consistent theory of both. We have to make a judgment on these things. Just because the two phenomena are inconsistent doesn't mean they're wrong. It means we don't understand them yet.

So, anyone who wants to believe that the Creator, or Spirit, or God can't exist, but believes in both gravity and quantum mechanics, is not being any more logical than someone who wants to believe that God does exist. Both are accepting things that are inconsistent. In science, we tend to push the inconsistencies under the rug and not talk about them. But they're there.

The question of free will is another inconsistency in science. According to the laws of physics, human beings can have no free will. Yet many scientists assume they have free will, that they are responsible for what they're doing and that they have choice. They may not believe in religion, but they believe they have free will, which they can't defend at all.

With science, we can do overt experiments. That's what makes so many people believe science really is *it*, and nothing else counts. We can repeat our experiments. Somebody else can repeat them. We seem to agree, and so on. But in some cases, scientists can't do experiments. Let's take astronomy, for example. We can only look and see what's there. We can't go out and play with the stars and push them around and make a new one and then have somebody else do it. We can only observe.

The same is true of most religious phenomena. We observe people. We observe history. We ask, what makes a good life? What do we admire? We use those observations to conclude, well, what is life, really? Does it have purpose? Does it have meaning? So, in both science and religion, we have observations.

We also have faith. Most people think faith is religious only, that it has nothing to do with science. Oh, as scientists we have to have a lot of faith. We have faith that the laws we find are constant, that they'll always be here. We don't know that. We test them and they seem to be here now, but who knows what'll happen tomorrow? We have to have a faith that the laws we discover are reliable. It's the same faith that there is a reliable God we can trust and believe in.

On the other hand, there has been one important difference between science and religion, and that is—science explores the universe and says what the universe is like. What science finds is there is there, and nothing else is there. There's no way of God intervening in anything, and there can be no moment of creation. Those ideas go back to the nineteenth century, when physicists thought everything was deterministic. They thought everything that happens is dependent on the past and is predictable from the past. As quantum mechanics was discovered, however, scientists found that things are not completely deterministic. There are uncertainties. Something new and uncontrollable can happen.

What is God like? To me, God is omnipresent and really quite personal. I pray regularly and I feel that interaction. Just as I feel I have free will, I feel God is there. I'm much dependent on him. I feel great help and support.

I had a remarkable experience in the fifties. Just sitting on a park bench, I had a breakthrough idea that led to the laser. I was chairman of a committee that tried to understand how to produce very short waves, short microwaves. As short as, maybe, a millimeter. We traveled all over the United States talking with people and looking at ideas. We weren't getting very far. I went to Washington for a meeting and was worried over this.

I got up early in the morning before this meeting. I went out to a nearby park, Franklin Park, and sat down on a bench. It was a nice spring morning, azaleas all out and beautiful. I sat there and thought, "Now, why haven't we been able to get somewhere with this?"

I thought, "Well, we just can't build things that are small enough to do this. Of course, we ought to use molecules, because molecules have frequencies like this in them. But because there's a thermodynamic law which says molecules can't produce any sizable amount of energy—"

I thought, "Well, now, wait, wait, wait. Wait a minute now. The molecules don't have to obey that law. Thermodynamics assumes you have a temperature. You don't have to have a temperature. So, wait a minute. Yeah. You can do that." And I immediately thought of how to put it all together and make a system where you could get radiation from the molecules. And that was the maser.

It was amazing, you know, amazing. Moses, the Buddha, all these people struggle with ideas and struggle with problems and then suddenly they have a revelation. You can sit under a bo tree or you can be wandering in the desert thinking about it, and suddenly there's some bush that strikes your attention and an idea comes.

So revelation is present in science also. I think many scientists recognize that they suddenly have ideas. Many would say it's a revelation. But if they don't want to believe in God, they would say, well, it just came to me. But one can take the attitude that God is in everything we do. God is all-pervasive. That's more or less the way I feel. God is omnipresent. He's here all the time. All of these things are God's doing.

God has been very dependable in my life. As I say, it's almost as instinctive as my sense that I have free will. I think I can make certain choices and I feel very strongly the presence of God. I feel that, yes, God is here. I can count on him. I think life is consistent with God's presence and with moral values. That's my best judgment.

PART THREE: *Holy Thunderbolts*

5

"My Sandwiches Said, 'Go Preach!'"

Charles Townes relies on observation and his own good judgment to arrive at his Christian trust in God. Anthony Mack says that without empirical evidence he can't believe in God at all. But dozens of other people I have met along the way—sensible, down-to-earth people—have very different stories to tell. They are stories not of thoughtful judgment or scientific evidence, but of a firsthand experience of the holy—of God, Nirvana, Spirit—breaking through and making itself known. It wasn't scientific knowledge, it was spiritual knowledge. And most often it came out of nowhere, unbidden, a holy thunderbolt.

For most of the many years I worked on this book I held out hope that sooner or later I too would be struck by a thunderbolt of my own, that the God of the outlet beach would show up again somehow and let me know of its reality in no uncertain terms. And for years, I labored under the assumption that this project would not be finished until I could offer my readers a brilliant insight, a vision of God that would bring this story to some kind of forceful, unequivocal end. Without such an epiphany, I would have nothing to say to my readers, I'd be wasting my time and theirs. I needed a punctuation mark from God, a crisp period to put at the end of this manuscript, my years of work, and the hours and hours of conversation.

But that was not to be. I experienced no thunderbolts along the way, no shattering insights, no holy visions fresh from heaven. And now I am realizing that, in my case, this state of affairs is totally fitting; I personally am not into thunderbolts. Not really.

Some people are. In observing people as a religion reporter and writer, I have noticed over the years that people often tend toward one spiritual temperament or another. Some prefer piety—loving devotion to God. Hindu tradition calls this the *bhakti* path. Others want nothing more than to serve their fellow humans and the world—the *karma* path in the Hindu tradition. Still others are meditators, able to retreat from the world for long hours in hopes of apprehending Spirit in a way that is beyond words—the *raja* path.

The fourth type of person, the thinker, the intellectual, the theologian, philosopher, and rabbi, the individual who is on what some traditions call the *jnana* path, likes to reflect on things. For these people, thunderbolts are not necessary. They like to observe, and arrive at—if not an ecstatic, sensual experience of the numinous—then a calm, sensible, thoughtful posture that, yes, God is here. God's sanctifying presence is everywhere.

That's me.

I noticed that what I enjoyed most as I listened to the wonderful stories that found their way into this book as well as the many I couldn't squeeze in—what I loved most was hearing the stories, studying them, wrestling with them, shaping them. I felt I was interviewing God—looking for and finding God in people's lives, often in ways that they hadn't quite seen for themselves. These stories were everywhere in abundance, and I liked sitting on the sidelines mulling them.

I'm reminded of the Reverend René Laurentin, a French priest and Mariologist I encountered on the religion beat at the *Contra Costa Times*. Born in Tours in 1917, Laurentin has made a career of investigating people who claim to have had apparitions of the Virgin Mary, including the visionaries of Medjugorje, whose tiny village in Bosnia and Herzegovina is now a famous pilgrimage site, attracting millions. Laurentin has written many books over the years, including *Bernadette Speaks* and *The Truth of Christmas*.

During our interview I asked Laurentin whether he'd ever seen the Virgin Mary for himself. No, he said, and he hoped he never would. If Mary were to appear to him, he'd lose his objectivity and then he wouldn't be able to do his job anymore, and Laurentin loved his job.

That's me. I love this job I have assigned myself. I love hearing and retelling the stories of other people's encounters with God. Much as I wouldn't mind a firsthand glimpse of the divine, what I really want to do right here and right now is what I'm already doing—recording and retelling other people's experiences.

Some of my interviewees told me that their luminous thunderbolt moments happened while they were reading scripture or participating in a formal worship service. But others reported that God revealed itself in the commonplace: in a sandwich at lunchtime or a pair of shoes getting wet in the rain.

Orenzia Bernstine tells one such story.

Born in Louisiana, the twelfth son of an African American plantation owner, Orenzia served in World War II then migrated west, settling in the industrial, seaport city of Richmond on the San Francisco Bay. There, he emerged as a moral and political force in the community, serving as a laborer, preacher, planning commissioner, and on the executive committee of the city's Unit-

ed Christian Democrats. He also pastored a series of thriving con-
gregations in Richmond, including the New St. James Missionary
Baptist Church, which at the time of our interview was affiliated
loosely with the National Baptist Convention, U.S.A.

I first heard about Orenzia during an election year. My editor
at the *Contra Costa Times* assigned some of us to write a story about local pastors who preach politics from the pulpit, and
Orenzia Bernstine fit right in. "I am always talking about being a
child of God," he told us. "And I'm always talking about being a
Democrat."

Later, when I began work on this book, I telephoned Orenzia
and arranged for an interview. On a sunny day in July, we sat
together at a small desk in the tiny foyer of the New St. James
Church in the heart of one of Richmond's African American
neighborhoods. Orenzia, seventy-eight on the day of our interview, wore a navy suit and a pale pink dress shirt. Thickly padded
ski gloves warmed his hands, which ached despite the summer
heat. Orenzia moved with the deliberateness of his years, but he
spoke effortlessly, in the rhythms of the Southern evangelist.

I had come prepared to talk politics. Instead, our conversation
turned to Orenzia's dramatic encounters with God. Like that of
the biblical prophet Jonah, Orenzia's story involves a dunking in
the salty waters of the Mediterranean. It begins in the South, during the Great Depression.

Orenzia Bernstine—His Story

My daddy was a preacher in hard times. He was an evangelist;
he traveled all over the country, preaching every night. He'd go
out, and come back home with all of his clothing just wet with
perspiration. There was no money in preaching then. They'd give
him a chicken, couple of heads of cabbage, and that was it. But my
God, when that man preached a revival, two and three hundred

souls would come to Christ, and that was rewards for him. He didn't care about no money.

My daddy had his own plantation in Natchitoches, Louisiana, three hundred acres. He grew cotton, corn, cane, all types of vegetables, cows, hogs, and horses. That plantation went way back in the family. My great-grandparents were farmers and they passed it on down to my grandfather and my daddy.

I accepted Christ at the age of eleven. My dad was running a revival at our church, the New Nazarene Missionary Baptist Church near Natchitoches, and I went to all of the services. One day it was raining and I was alone in my daddy's barn where the horses and cows would be fed, and I said to the Lord, "Lord, I know that if I die now I'm going to hell because I do know right from wrong. I want you to save me today or kill me and let me go on to hell."

God came into my life at that moment. I started praising the Lord and singing, and when I looked around, that barn was full of people. They heard me singing. Momma came running. Daddy came. And here come all the deacons of the church. They all come running, they heard Orenzia had accepted Christ. But how in the world did they get the word? That has always been a mystery to me. No telephone, nothing but trees, and all of those people are in this barn, and I'm jumping from one person to the other. I was on fire and I was setting everybody on fire that I touched.

I went to the church that night. I had to tell my testimony, which was the best thing that could happen to people back in those days. I got up to tell my testimony and I started walking on the shoulders of people. I walked on my daddy's shoulders and on the deacons' shoulders, just walking from one shoulder to the other—and never fell. I was doing everything but fly in that church.

My daddy was crying. He said to the people, "You have heard

the statement coming from my son. What is your pleasure?"

And all the deacons stood up. "Brother Pastor, I make the motion that Orenzia become a member of this church." And everybody in the church said, "Amen!" Outside they were saying, "Amen!" I felt that with the Lord there was nothing I couldn't do.

At the age of thirteen, the Lord inspired me to preach. I was babysitting my brother's children, the babies were asleep, and I was praying and singing.

> *Wherever I go, I'm going to tell it.*
> *Be me high or be me low,*
> *I'm gonna tell it wherever I go.*

And the Lord spoke. He said, "I want you to preach."

I stopped singing. I said, "Say, what?"

"I want you to preach."

It was a real voice. It looked like it come from this corner over here. I turned and I said, "What?"

"I want you to preach."

Then it began to unravel to me, and I said, "Oh, Lord, I don't want to be a preacher. Why would you want me to preach when my daddy has been a preacher and he ain't never got nothing but hard work, perspiration running out of his shoes?"

But the Lord meant it. I didn't tell nobody, I didn't do nothing but ponder over that till I got to my momma. I said, "Momma, I got something to tell you, but you got to promise me that you won't tell nobody."

She said, "I know what it is."

I said, "What is it?"

"The Lord has anointed you to preach."

I said, "That's it. But please don't tell nobody."

The Lord was so patient with me, he put up with so much with me. I went into the Army in 1941, World War II. My first night on the ship when I was going overseas, he appeared to me, he said, "Step up in my hand."

And I stepped up in his hands.

And he said, "I want you to know, he who I hold in the palm of my hand, I'll defy all the devils in hell to pluck him out." He said, "Don't worry, no bodily harm is coming to you."

I had the bombs fall all around me out there, not a shrapnel scratched me nowhere. Nowhere. I have one scratch. A guy was trying to put a bayonet in one of my friends, and I grabbed hold of the bayonet and hit him with my rifle. That's the only scratch that I got, was on my hand. I say to anybody, if you can't trust the Lord, you can't trust nothing. And I'll dare you to trust him. He has never failed me yet, and I've been in some tight spots with him.

I was in on the invasion of Italy. They were sending us on a Navy freight-carrying ship from Sicily to the Anzio beachhead. On our way, our ship got torpedoed, and I lost pretty near three hundred of my compadres. It was a black outfit, a division. I was among the last three people to leave the ship. The captain, the executive officer, and myself. I was helping others to get off. The ship was sinking, and the holds were filling with water, and I saw a mattress floating there. I put a rope around it and threw it off the ship, and I jumped in the water. I put my arm around the rope so I could rest my chin on my arm and keep my head from going under water, and I held on tight with my hands, and my hands never did get over that. Then the boiler exploded and that was it. I laid out there with that mattress in that water for nine-and-a-half hours.

I had to surrender to the Lord. I said, "Whatever you want me to do, whatever you want me to say, to whoever you want me to say it to, I'll do it, if you'll just let somebody come and get me."

About three or four minutes after I said that, there was a light way over yonder, shining on me. People coming, English people. They looked down. "Hello, mate." You know how they talk. "How are you doing down there?"

I said, "I guess I'm okay."

He said, "Tell you what I'm going do, old mate. I'm going to come down, I'm going to put a belt around you, and we going to draw you up."

I said, "Thank you, Jesus." And they did that.

When I got to the deck of the ship, he said, "Look at that bloody mattress. It is going down like a bloody piece of cement. What was holding it up, old mate?"

I said, "Eternal God that holds the whole world in his hands."

He said, "Man, I got to believe in it, because I've seen with my own eyes."

Why would a mattress float? Because God saved me for this day to talk to you. And that's my real feelings about God.

After I got discharged from the Army, I came out here to Richmond and got married. I was working for J.H. Fitzmaurice in Oakland, a concrete contractor. My wife was having babies, one every two years. I had to do a lot of pondering. I had to think about the promise I had made to the Lord. The Lord was calling me to preach, but I had to stay there on that job and work to support my family.

At J.H. Fitzmaurice, I worked up off the ground, way up above the concrete mixer. One day I went to work, and my work was pressing on me. I went up the steps on this Monday morning. I said, "My Lord, if you really want me to preach, I want you to let the sun be hidden by a cloud."

A cloud came up, hid the sun from me.

I said, "Now, Lord, listen to me. If you really want me to

preach, move the cloud. That's all, move the cloud."

It cleared up. The sun was shining beautiful.

Still, I just didn't want to preach. So I came down for lunch. I usually went to the room where everybody else was eating. I wouldn't go. I sat on the steps, trying to open my lunch box.

I opened it.

Sandwich said, "Go preach!"

I closed it up. Opened it again.

"Go preach!"

Closed it up. I wouldn't open it no more. Just sat there.

The man that I was working with, he came up. He said, "Bernstine, did you eat your lunch?"

Pretended I didn't hear him.

He said, "Bernstine, did you eat your lunch?"

I said, "No. I can't eat no lunch."

He said, "What's the matter?"

I said, "All my sandwiches are saying, 'Go preach!'"

So I ran to the superintendent's office. I guess I looked so stupid, the superintendent said, "What is the matter with you?"

I said, "The Lord has called me to preach."

The superintendent was Robert Fitzmaurice, one of the owner's sons. He said, "You go preach, man. Go preach!"

I left work. Got in my car. All the way down that highway, from Oakland to Richmond, I preached. I had the windows down low and I was preaching. Some people laughed. I said, "Laugh if you want. I'm telling you what the Lord has told me to tell you. Repent of your sins on this day."

I went home and I told my wife. She said, "Well, if that's what it is, that's what it is."

I said, "That's it. I have told the Lord I'm going to do it, and there ain't nothing going to stop me from doing it, Baby, I mean nothing."

I stayed off that job three weeks. I had to walk this community here in Richmond to let people know that the Lord had anointed me to preach. And I didn't lose a penny. J.H. Fitzmaurice paid me for every day that I was off.

After that, the Lord always made a way for me. I organized a church, and was pastoring that church and making my own living working full time at the Concord Naval Weapons Station, teaching people how to handle ammunition. Sometimes I had two other jobs. Then I got my back hurt at work; they wouldn't let me go back, so I got disability payments from the federal government. That was a blessing to me; I didn't have to depend on the church to take care of me. The Lord just said, "This is it. Your preaching is your full-time job, and I'm going to take care of you."

I've been at it now for fifty years. Fifty years have taught me a lesson. I don't care what they give me, I'm going to preach. I wouldn't take nothing for my life as a preacher. I wouldn't take nothing but heaven for it, and that's where I'm going.

6

Meeting Jesus

Mark Zapalik had not anticipated, or even wanted, a sign from God. He wasn't looking for a conversion experience when he agreed to go to church with his wife and her friends one summer afternoon. He went because they'd promised him music, and he was a music-loving kind of guy. Little did he know that the service would change his life forever, causing him to give up "sex, drugs, and rock 'n' roll" for the love of Jesus Christ and, eventually, to trade in a good-paying job for conservative politics.

Mark went on to become Contra Costa County's foremost spokesman for the Christian right. At the time of our earliest interviews, he was director of the county's Traditional Values Coalition and opposed to abortion, euthanasia, gun control, gay men as Boy Scout leaders, and special legal protections for gays, lesbians, and people with AIDS. He defended prayer in the public schools, school vouchers, and parental rights. His bulldog tenacity when it came to causes he believed in was legendary among local citizens, their elected officials, and the newspaper reporters—myself included—who encountered him on their beats.

At the time, Mark was living in Brentwood, a farm town on the Sacramento River Delta that was briskly transforming itself into a middle class suburb. His long, uneasy relationship with the local media had left him wary of newspaper reporters. And so, rather than invite me into his home for our interviews, Mark suggested we meet at Sylvia's Country Kitchen in nearby Antioch.

A broad-shouldered, muscular man with dark, curly hair, olive skin, and a salt-and-pepper beard, Mark was at ease in this coffee shop setting. He bantered with our waitresses—we talked through at least two of their shifts—and he was careful to thank them for each coffee refill and each plate of food set before him.

Those restaurant conversations spanned seven months and several hearty meals. Mark pulled no punches. Like many born-again Christians, he was willing to talk about the misguided life he had led before his dramatic first encounter with Jesus. He laid his political opinions on the table without apology and, with great relish, he told the story of how he came to be Contra Costa's most conservative political gadfly.

"God had his thumb on me," he said of his decision to go to work for the Traditional Values Coalition, leaving behind a promising, high-paid career in the transportation industry. "America is not the America it was. I'm fighting desperately to restore what we've lost."

Over the years, the two of us—the ultra-conservative political activist and the liberal to moderate journalist—have come to respect one another. Mark touches me with his warmth, honesty, and the thoughtful moral accountability he imposes upon himself. He likes me, I hope, for my willingness to hear and retell his story as he experiences it.

Mark's story begins with a small child.

Mark Zapalik—His Story

The orphanage was called St. Joseph's home for the friendless, and the only thing I remember about it is sitting on the floor with a bunch of other kids, looking up at a black-and-white TV with rabbit ears, watching "Howdy Doody."

It was a Catholic institution in Chicago and a good place probably, because when my parents adopted me, I was very polite. I said please and thank you, so I was well trained by somebody. I remember meeting my parents; they came to the orphanage several times, and we sat in a room with a little airplane and some toys and we talked. I was three-and-a-half.

I had been given up to the orphanage at age three. I don't know anything about the first three years of my life. I have no memory, and I have never found anybody who could fill in the blanks. I don't know who my birth mother was beyond the name on the original birth certificate and that I was born in Chicago on February 3, 1953.

My new parents lived in Cicero, Illinois, a suburb west of Chicago. They were Catholic and they sent me to a Catholic grade school two blocks from our house. The Catholic Church made it clear that God loved and cared for his children. It also taught that if you sin, you break God's heart and he cries, and the angels cry, and that if you do too much of that you won't go to heaven. I didn't have a problem with God as a little boy. I knew there was something big about God. I prayed to him when I needed things and when I was in trouble. But the religiosity of the Catholic Church, the ritual, was so impersonal that I didn't feel God was close to me, or I to him.

I was a strong-willed child and a hell-raiser in school. I was constantly pushing against my parents and against authority, testing the limits. I found out a lot later in life that I was testing to see if there was a line I would not be allowed to cross. If I could find that line, I would feel safe. I felt abandoned by my biological mother. No matter what I had, it could be taken away in an instant, even my parents. I could be back at the orphanage at any time. I didn't feel safe in love.

The first time I fell in love, I was twelve years old. I saved a bunch of money, two dollars maybe, and I bought a little ring with a stone in it. I walked over to the little girl's house and asked her to go steady. She said no. I went home and I lay on my bed and I cried and cried and cried. My mom wanted to know what was wrong. When I told her, she said I was way too young to be in love and I was silly for even thinking about it.

That was it. I ran away from home. I took whatever money I had in my desk drawer and jumped on my bicycle. I rode to the CTA train station, locked my bike to the fence, and took the train to Chicago. When I got downtown, I found a phone booth and a phone book, and I looked for St. Joseph's Home for the Friendless. I was going to go to this orphanage and find out where my mother was. I couldn't find it in the phone book, so I bought a soda with the money I had left and I sat there on a bench for hours. Finally, I called home. I had run out of money so I had to sneak back onto the train. My mom and dad were waiting in the car for me at the station.

I had to settle for life the way it was. I couldn't run home to Mom, whoever she was. I wasn't going to find her without intervention from an adult, and I didn't think my parents would help me look for her. I would have to deal with the bumps and defeats on my own. I wanted that connection to Mom, to something, but at that age I couldn't make it happen. It was a bigger project than I knew how to handle.

I left the Catholic Church at fourteen. I didn't need God, I had better things to do. I believed God was there and I knew I was going to be accountable. But, hey, I was fifteen and I had a hundred years before I needed to worry about that.

I got into sports in high school and did well diving for the swimming team, which got me a lot of respect. I moved with the jocks and the cheerleaders. The summer after my freshman year, I found some older guys who were into drugs, and it wasn't long before they were sharing with me. I found a whole new world of excitement, sneaking around doing what I wanted. I was into Jimi Hendrix, the Moody Blues, the Beatles, mind expanding. I showed up for school my sophomore year wearing brown penny loafers and corduroys—and a black Naugahyde trench coat with all the pockets, which was what the hard guys were into. I didn't know where I belonged.

Then I met the girl who became my wife. We went on a date, and, man, she was perfect. We were in love, the whole thing. We finished high school and went to college. When I was nineteen, I dropped out of college, got a full-time job with a steamship company, and my first apartment, my own place. We decided to get married.

But for me, it always came back to being able to take off at any time and, metaphorically, look for Mom. As much as I loved my wife and wanted her, there was still this empty hole, something wasn't right, I needed something more. I did drugs and ran around with the wrong crowd. Friday night was the guys' night out. It was the seventies, and it was fine to go to a disco and dance with women who weren't necessarily your wife. Some of the guys took it further than that. I didn't. But, gosh, I wanted something, and I didn't know what it was.

We had a forest preserve near us with picnic benches and grass meadows for playing ball. Some nights I hung out there with the boys and some of their girls. I encouraged my wife to come along, because I didn't want to give up one for the other. But that wasn't her scene. She didn't like that stuff. And before long we were divorced.

A lot of guys my age went to Vietnam. I didn't. I had broken my wrist playing ball when I was a kid and it was supposed to be in the cast six or seven weeks. Me, I take the cast off after two weeks. It was summer, and I just slipped my arm out of it so I could get back to diving. My wrist never did heal right, and I couldn't rotate my wrist fully, so the Army 4F'd me. I kept busy. I rebuilt cars, Corvairs. I picked up a guitar and sang rock music. I was into all those things, yet something wasn't right, something was missing.

At work I heard about something called Transactional Analysis, which is a kind of psychotherapy. You know that book, *I'm OK, You're OK*? I wound up going into Transactional Analysis for almost three years. That's where I began to understand that a lot of my anger and emotional disconnect came from the sense I had no roots and that I had been abandoned as a small child.

For a while I wanted to find those roots, so I went through the Chicago phone books and made a lot of calls looking for my mom. When I found the orphanage, they couldn't help because the strict Illinois laws kept adoption records sealed. When I had exhausted all the easy ways of finding the person, I gave up the search. If I found my biological mother, it could be she was some slut who didn't care about me. Or it could be a heartbreak story about how she never wanted to give me up. Either way, I had no control over the past. I decided to pick myself up by the bootstraps and take who I was now and work with that.

I met a woman at work, Sherry, who was divorced and had two kids, a four-year-old boy and a nine-year-old girl. I moved in with her. Within a year, we were married. A lady Episcopalian priest administered the vows in a picnic grove with all our hippie friends. Two lesbian nuns sang and played the guitar.

Sherry and I moved to the San Francisco Bay Area in 1978. San Francisco's free spirit attracted me. If you wanted to dance in the streets, if you wanted to be gay, if you wanted to put on puppet shows or do drugs, there was no stigma. It was, hey, come as you are, do what you want, be free. I didn't have a political agenda, I wanted to be accepted, so I accepted everybody else's lifestyle. That's what drew me to San Francisco. Later, as the director of a Traditional Values Coalition chapter, I was often on talk shows or on the front line of a street protest, and somebody will blurt out that I'm uptight, that I don't know anything. If they only knew!

Sherry and I rented a house in Concord, and I went to work as a maintenance manager for Southern Pacific Railroad. It turned out that Sherry and I couldn't have children, but I enjoyed being a good stepfather to hers.

We got to be friends with a couple who went to the Concord Church of the Nazarene. I didn't want anything to do with a church, but Sherry went Sunday mornings, and I started practicing with the men's softball team. Eventually, I started going to church, too—I had to in order to play on their team. But Sherry was going every Sunday and liking it. One day while she was watching Pat Robertson's 700 Club on TV she heard a call from God. She asked the Lord into her heart, and she got "born again."

Now I had this religious zealot in the house. She started going to church Wednesday and Sunday nights as well as Sunday mornings. Pretty soon she was going to all the potlucks. When she was home, it was God this and God that. I tolerated it. I thought religion was fine for my wife. People had religion because they needed it, and that was okay with me. I didn't want to be judgmental.

One day, Sherry and her church friend invited me to go to services that Mario Murillo, an evangelist, was holding in the Oakland Auditorium. "They've got a live band," they said. "Real music. Bass guitar. Electric guitar. Synthesizers. A full drum kit. You'll like it." I said okay. We sat way in the back of the auditorium. The music wasn't Jimi Hendrix, but at least it wasn't some old hymn; it was upbeat. I didn't think church people got into stuff like that. It was cool.

The pastor talked about the difference between going through ritual and having a personal relationship with Jesus Christ. Some people feel empty, he said. They don't feel connected, and that's because they don't have that personal contact with God. I wasn't sure I wanted to believe this. I had shot off in directions before, thinking this was it or that was it. Now this preacher was inviting me to come down to the altar and meet the Lord Jesus Christ for myself.

I wanted to run away. Yet I had this longing, this sense of—home. This was the place. This was where I belonged—Mom or roots or womb. I wanted to run down that aisle and get there. I had to be there. This was what I had been looking for all these years. I wanted to go down there, and yet I wanted to run away.

The preacher said, "Right now, there is somebody here who has been wondering, where is this place? What is this relationship? Well, it's right here, right now."

I stood there, eyes closed. I was paralyzed. I was losing my hearing. The music, the preacher's voice, everything went down in volume, as if somebody had turned a knob on a radio. Finally I couldn't hear anything. I got scared. Had I passed out? Was I dreaming?

I opened my eyes. The room had faded to white. The reds had become pinkish. The room was bright. I couldn't see the stage. I could feel the seat in front of me. My wife was next to me, and there were people all around. But I couldn't see anything but white.

When I looked toward the stage, I saw Jesus Christ standing there, looking at me. His eyes were so deep, like the sea. I could have been floating a hundred feet underwater with nothing but sea a thousand miles in every direction. I was washed in peace and heat, from the tip of my head to the toes of my feet. He stood there in a white robe, his arms open, his eyes looking into mine. Only he and I were in the room. There was total peace. I had never experienced anything like it before. Not in the drugs, not in the sex, not in any of the things I had ever used to feel good. There was no comparison.

I started to move. I had to feel where the seats were because there was all this white. My wife and our friend moved aside. I'm sure they were ecstatic, thinking, "Oh, gosh. He's going to be saved." When I got to the aisle, I looked up and he was gone. I felt the peace, but I didn't see him. I could see the preacher and I could vaguely hear the music, but I wasn't paying attention. I just knew I had to get down there. That's where I belonged.

Jesus Christ was the peg that fit the hole I had been feeling all my life. I had thought the hole was not knowing my biological parents. I had wondered if there was something wrong with me that somebody didn't want me. There was this void I didn't know how to fill. God filled it, and now I know God is all I need. He is everything.

I've heard so many people in Christianity say, "I had the job. I had the wife. I had the house. I had the family. I had the car. I had it all, but I didn't have anything. Something was missing." And then, when they come into this relationship with Jesus, they live for him.

That was the day I met Jesus Christ. That was the beginning.

Now, years later, I know what a personal relationship with God is. I've had trials and tribulations in life since then, but I never have that feeling that I don't know where I belong or who I belong to. That has been settled. That was the day he called me home, and I went.

After that day, I went to the Nazarene church and I listened to what was said. I read the Bible and took it seriously. I gave up drugs and pornography. I gave up thoughts of extramarital affairs. I paid back people I had stolen things from. I even gave up all of my music collection. This was the new life God was calling me to and it made for considerable changes in my life.

Fortunately, I had already given up most of the drugs and booze when I got married and stepped these two kids. I still smoked marijuana a couple times a year, but nothing heavier. And I wasn't bingeing on alcohol like in the party days, when it would be nothing to get started Friday after work and then pull myself off the floor on Monday morning.

To get rid of the music was an effort. I had four or five hundred albums on shelves in the rec room, the original *Meet the Beatles* album, Diana Ross and the Supremes, Deep Purple, all the Hendrix albums, all the Pink Floyd, a lot of Yes albums, Santana. I had it all. There was the drug stuff—Jimi Hendrix's *Purple Haze*. The LSD stuff—the Beatles' *Lucy in the Sky with Diamonds*. The free love stuff—love the one you're with, if it feels right, do it. There are a lot of messages like that in music, and I was the kind who would listen.

Those songs had emotional connections for me. Listening to them took me back to the forest preserve with my buddies, getting high, getting drunk, figuring out what gals to hit on. Go to a motel or something. If I happen to hear that music now, it's okay. But I no longer buy it or feast on it. It would take my mind back into those times and those old attitudes.

I loaded my albums, hundreds of them, into my shag-carpeted, bed-in-the-back Dodge van and drove down to a place in Walnut Creek where they buy records. I took a shellacking. At the time, I didn't know the value of some of those albums. The *Meet the Beatles*, the original pressing, I didn't get much for it. It had its original poster insert and lyric sheet, and not a fingerprint on it. After that, Sherry and I started buying Christian contemporary music. Folk songs and light rock. Don Francisco and Maranatha.

I had a microphone at home I used to practice songs. One day I put on a music track to work on a song to sing in church. The intro was playing, and before I could sing a word, I looked at that mike and went, "You stole this microphone!" I had stolen it from a music shop in Chicago when I was twenty-four years old. When the owner went into the back room to get something, I reached around the cabinet, pulled the microphone out, and stuck it down the front of my pants. I knew if somebody saw it there, they wouldn't ask me about it. And off I went.

I called back to Chicago and got the address of the store. It was a hundred-and-twenty-five-dollar microphone, so I sent the manager something like a hundred and forty bucks along with a note explaining that I used to do things like this, but now I had found God through Jesus Christ. I never heard from him, but he did cash the check.

I wrestled with the pornography. I tried six ways to a dozen to justify keeping it. It's okay, I told myself, it's for my private use, I'm not passing it on to other people. It took everything I had to get it out of my life. I was never into the S&M stuff or the kiddie porn, but I had plenty of magazines and films from smut shops around Chicago. *Penthouse. Club. Hustler.* Eight-millimeter films of people having sex.

Even before I was a Christian I realized I had to put some brakes on myself, because pornography is addictive. You want to see more, you want something new. Two people having sex together isn't enough anymore. You want to see three people. You want to see increased numbers of people doing increased numbers of things. When four ways of having sex isn't enough, then what? It's not that physical sensuality between two committed, married people is a bad thing. The issue is the mindset. Am I loving you? Is the pleasure mutual? Or do I want this from you because it's got to look like that movie I watch?

I sat in our kitchen in Concord one day with all these reels of film stacked on the table, about a dozen of them. I pulled a garbage can over to the table and put a pencil through the middle of each reel. One by one, I spun the film off the reels into the garbage.

I did my best to live a clean life after that. I went to church. I worked hard at my job with the railroad. I was registered to vote. I thought I was fulfilling my civic duty, my Christian duty, my family duties. Then, one Sunday, I saw a big article in the Sunday newspaper about my city sponsoring a Gay Pride Week. I was upset; the Bible makes it clear that homosexual acts are against God's law. That's when I became active in the Traditional Values Coalition. It's a grassroots lobby that was focusing on homosexuality, along with abortion and euthanasia, pornography, parental rights, and freedom of religious expression in schools and the public square. A few years later, I left my railroad job to take over as director of the Contra Costa TVC chapter.

Each TVC chapter is self-sustaining financially. The donations aren't that much. Some months, by the time I paid for the phone, the fax, and the postage and printing, there was nothing left over and I didn't get paid. By the time I left the TVC, I'd sacrificed a half-million dollars or more of earning potential.

Why are those issues so important to me? Because America is not the America it was. We have been headed in the right direction on civil rights and women's issues, but now others are co-opting the reasoning and good intentions behind those movements. The new public mindset is we have to be non-judgmental. Sexual promiscuity is okay, pornography is okay, abortion is okay. But making moral judgments is not okay.

When I was forty-three years old, Sherry died of breast cancer. It was lonely after she was gone. I was only forty-three, and being alone got way too difficult. Bars were a temptation. When I drove by one, I thought, why not go in and socialize. Dance a little. Have a 7UP. Listen to the music and watch the people.

But I knew it would be playing with fire spiritually. Things could happen. I could wake up the next morning someplace I didn't want to be. How would I reconcile that with God and my community? Several times a week I was fighting that steering wheel. The Bible says it's not good for a man to be alone, and now I knew why.

I had never dated as a Christian. Everything I knew about getting things started was from this other world, my old life. So I ordered up some of the church books and videotapes they make for teenagers. Here I was, a man in my forties, reading about what's proper and improper, moral and immoral. But it was fun. I felt God was giving me the time of my life. When I was a teenager I had cheated myself out of the opportunity to do it God's way. Now I was getting a second chance.

I set up my own hybrid plan with one strict rule: no physical contact with a woman unless we were courting—courting meaning that we were dating only one another and we had marriage in mind. If I dated more than one woman at a time, I might be hugging and kissing and stuff with one, and then a couple nights later doing the same with another.

I listed myself on a Christian dating service and in the newspaper. "Christian widower in search of single Christian woman." My prayer to God was, "I want who you want for me. Not the perfect woman, but the person you would hand-select for me."

A widow, Susan, saw the newspaper listing and contacted me. About three months later, we got married at my home church, Oak Park Assembly in Pleasant Hill. Sadly, that marriage didn't last, but it produced two sons, Nathan and Jacob. Because Sherry and I had not been able to have children, I had figured that in God's economy my stepson and stepdaughter—who are now adult Christians raising kids of their own—would be my blessing of children to enjoy and raise. But God is so overwhelmingly kind and generous. He gave me not one, but two sons of my own.

Ever since that day—since that service in the Oakland Auditorium—God has been there for me. Which is why I must do all I can to actively support my boys. I spent years trying to figure out why I was so angry and what was missing and why I couldn't feel whole or complete. And I thought for so long that it was because I didn't know my mom. I didn't know who she was or why she had left me at that orphanage. But when I found the Lord, I realized that I was God's child and he was everything. I feel complete in him. I don't feel that emptiness any more. That need, that drive, that want, that hole I was trying to fill, just got washed away.

I want to be a father in my boys' lives the way God has been a father in my life. I don't want them to ever have that feeling I had of being abandoned. I want to be there for them. I want to go to their football games. I want to take them to church and pray with them and teach them all I can about God. My boys are such a total joy. God has richly blessed me. God is good.

7

Epiphany in the Schoolyard

Sister Barbara Hazzard used to be a Holy Names sister. Now she's a Benedictine monastic. She began her life as a Catholic religious at the age of seventeen when she took vows with a teaching order, the Sisters of the Holy Names of Jesus and Mary. Nearly three decades later, after much soul-searching, Sister Barbara left the Holy Names sisters and joined the monastic community of the Order of St. Benedict.

It was in her calling as a Benedictine that Sister Barbara founded Hesed, a community devoted to bringing Christ-centered meditation into the lives of busy urban Christians. Located in the First Congregational Church of Oakland, Hesed is part of the World Community for Christian Meditation founded by Father Laurence Freeman in the tradition of John Main and the Rule of St. Benedict. Hesed's innovative week-day evening meditation and prayer services attract Christians—often lay people with jobs and families—from all over the San Francisco Bay Area and the world.

When I first interviewed Sister Barbara, Hesed was located in a small, stucco bungalow in the Glenview district of Oakland, where most houses on the block were home to families and working people. Hesed's main floor housed a kitchen, living room, dining room, office, and bedrooms for Sister Barbara and over-night visitors on retreat from the work-a-day world. Downstairs, in what used to be a basement, was a meditation room furnished with mats and cushions. Next to it, a small sanctuary sheltered an altar and the consecrated Eucharist.

Sister Barbara has kept her own life simple and informal. On the day of our first interview, she wore khaki pants, a cotton shirt, and brand-new white canvas Keds. Her straight hair was cropped short across her forehead, ears, and neck. Her skin—soft, pink, and flawless— hinted at her previous life as a Catholic sister living in a convent and teaching school. It was the complexion of a woman who'd had little use for sunbathing for most of her sixty-plus years.

When Sister Barbara talks about her life as a Catholic religious, first as a sister and now as a monastic, it is with quiet joy and clarity about her calling. She traces that clarity to a pivotal moment—a holy thunderbolt akin to those of Orenzia and Mark—years ago as she stood under a willow tree in a Los Angeles schoolyard.

I found Sister Barbara's conversational style as modest as her appearance. She was not one to talk glibly about herself or her spiritual life, and it took several visits to the Hesed bungalow to pull the story of Sister Barbara's thunderbolt moment from her reticent lips.

Sister Barbara Hazzard—Her Story

As a child, I never dreamed I'd take vows as a Holy Names sister, let alone as a Benedictine. I was much too independent-minded. When I was in first grade, for instance, I signed my own report card and turned it back in to the teacher. I couldn't understand why my mother was so upset.

"Why shouldn't I sign it?" I said. "It's my report card."

My father had the same mischievous nature and he egged me on. His name was William Henry Hazzard, but everybody called him Hap Hazzard. He wanted me to look at things in a fresh way and not just accept other people's ideas of how things should be. Whenever I got into trouble, which was pretty often, he stood up for me.

Even though he was a Presbyterian, my father was on good terms with the sisters at my Catholic grammar school and high school, and he was famous for his practical jokes. He particularly liked to play tricks on Sister Emily Marie, the treasurer of my high school, which was run by the Sisters of the Holy Names of Jesus and Mary. When my parents dropped me off at school one day, my father handed me a cloth bag filled with something heavy. "Here," he said. "Give this to Sister Emily Marie. Tell her it's your tuition." When Sister Emily opened the bag, she laughed. It was a bank bag, full of pennies.

I experienced the Sisters of the Holy Names for the first time in 1949, when I was in the eighth grade. My family had moved to Pasadena and I was sent to St. Elizabeth's, which was one of their schools. Although I was an eighth grader, I found myself drawn to the third grade teacher at my new school, Sister Margaret Mary. This was her first year of teaching, or close to it, and she was different from any sister I had ever met. She was young and pretty and had a lot of energy and she seemed to really enjoy life. I'd see her out on the schoolyard during recess, playing with the kids and laughing out loud.

The sisters still wore their black habits in those days. They were long-sleeved, full-length affairs with a black veil and a starched white linen bandeau and coif around the face. Underneath the habit, the sisters had these big aprons with deep, deep pockets, which they could reach into through slits in the outer skirt. The sisters didn't carry purses at the time, so everything went into those pockets: scissors, school supplies, first-aid kits, etc. They were like little saddlebags.

Sister Margaret Mary liked to play kickball with the kids, but she didn't just watch, she actually pitched the ball and ran the bases. She was fun, but she was also beautiful to look at. She had dark eyes and a round, lively, smiling face. Her hands were beautiful too, strong, but feminine and lovely. That's all you could see of Sister Margaret Mary in the habit she wore—her face and her hands.

I got a big crush on her, the way girls that age will do with a young teacher they admire, and I would go over to her classroom after school to help grade papers and clean the blackboards, etc. We talked a lot and got to be friends, as much as our age difference and her status as a professed sister and mine as an eighth grader would allow. Each afternoon around four o'clock, I'd walk her across the school grounds to the convent where she lived. Then I'd catch the bus to my house and be home in time to practice the piano and do my homework before dinner. I was a pretty good student in those days and I thought I might work in a hospital as a surgical nurse when I grew up.

The architecture of my school was Spanish, with tile roofs, stucco walls, and bathrooms that opened onto the schoolyard. It was Sister Margaret Mary's duty to lock up the bathroom doors every afternoon before she went back to the convent. One day, when four o'clock rolled around, we looked outside and saw that it was raining really hard. She opened one of those big, black umbrellas that the nuns always seemed to have, and the two of us walked together across the yard.

There were puddles everywhere, so I stopped under a great weeping willow tree to wait while Sister took the umbrella and went ahead to lock up. I was wearing my school uniform that day, a royal blue cotton dress with pleats in the skirt, a stiff white collar, and a white necktie. Silk scarves were popular in those days, and that morning I had tied a bright-colored scarf around my neck.

I was watching Sister make her way through the puddles when I noticed something—she had a hole in the sole of her shoe. Now, technically speaking, this was not Sister Margaret Mary's shoe. In the convent, everything was communal. It was our book. Our pencil. And, in this case, our shoe.

Without thinking, I shouted out, "Hey, Sister, you have a hole in our shoe."

That was a very bold thing for an eighth grade girl to say to a sister in 1950. In those days you didn't tease with the sisters. It was a pretty formal relationship, and this little joke of mine was pushing the limits. Sister and I had kidded around a lot, but this was the first time I had kidded about something so personal. I wondered if I had taken things too far. If she ignored my remark, I thought, it would be her signal to me that I had overstepped, and I would have to be more circumspect next time.

But Sister Margaret Mary didn't ignore me or my little joke. She turned around, looked right at me, laughed, and gave me one of her beautiful smiles.

"What a wonderful person," I thought. "How I'd love to be like that."

A light went on.

"Oh, my God!" I said to myself. "What am I saying?"

I had never thought about being a nun. I was too much of a renegade for that. Besides, I was planning to be a surgical nurse. But now, whoa! A sister? I was awestruck.

Sister Margaret Mary turned away and continued across the schoolyard to the bathrooms. I just stood there under the willow tree in wonder, feeling the rain dripping off the tree onto my hair and my uniform.

Something happened to me under that tree that day. Something beautiful and hopeful. I couldn't put it into words then, or even now. It wasn't a thought. It was a feeling that went deep into my body. I walked her back to the convent as usual, but I hardly said a word the whole way. Then I headed home on foot. I didn't want to ride the bus with all those people and all that racket. Something had happened, and I wanted time to be with it. The walk was a long one in the downpour, but I didn't mind. I hardly noticed the rain.

I was almost an hour late getting home and I was soaking wet when I got there. My uniform was soggy and limp. The dye from my silk scarf had run and stained my white collar with bright splotches of color. My mother had been waiting for me and when she saw me coming up the front walk she met me at the door. She was a loving mother who ran a beautiful home, but she was sort of a worrywart.

"Where have you been?" she said.

"I walked home."

I brushed past her and went to my room. No explanation. No apology. I was so completely taken by this new idea that I'd had under the willow tree . . . and it wasn't my idea, I'll tell you that.

My mother followed me into my room. "Are you okay?"

"Yeah. I'm fine."

She studied me for a moment; then, satisfied that I was all right, she left the room. I put my books down, went into the kitchen for something to eat, and life went on as usual. For the next several weeks, I just lived with this new idea. I was still just an eighth grader, but I wrote to the provincial administration of the Sisters of the Holy Names up in Los Gatos for information. When my mother saw the stuff coming in the mail, she put two and two together. She had gone to school to the Sisters of the Holy Names in Oregon and she was a mother, so she knew. She could see the change in me, but she didn't say anything. My father, he didn't want to know.

My desire to be a sister never left me. I did all the normal things that kids do. I dated in high school and when I was a senior I had a steady boyfriend. Privately I knew what I was going to do. It all came out into the open during my senior year when I bought a pair of oxfords and had them dyed. My parents and I were sitting around the kitchen table having breakfast, and the shoes, regulation brown Girl Scout shoes dyed black, were sitting there in their shoebox, ready to go to the convent with me when I graduated.

My father spotted them. "Well," he said. "What are these?" He suspected, of course, but he wanted to hear it from me.

"I'm going to need them when I go into the convent," I said as gently as I could.

He couldn't talk. He got up from the table and went out the kitchen door to the back yard, where he liked to work on the weekends. It was then, I think, that he realized this was really going to happen. I followed him outside and talked with him for a while. But I was young and I couldn't see how tough this was going to be on him and on my mother.

I graduated from high school that June, and in July the three of us drove the four hundred miles north to the novitiate in Los Gatos. We had to make a stop on the way on account of my hair. One of the requirements of the novitiate was that if your hair was long, which mine was, it had to be parted in the middle and braided on the sides so that it would fit under the postulant's hair net. I wasn't used to wearing my hair that way, so we had to stop at the hairdresser's to have it done.

We were a little late in arriving as a result. The novitiate was large, pinkish-tinged, and set with some other buildings on eight or nine acres of beautiful lawn and gardens. No sooner was I out of the car than one of the sisters stepped up to greet me. "Okay, Barbara," she said. "Come with me." She swished me through the front door, leaving my mother and father behind in the garden.

Inside, a half dozen sisters waited in the vestibule to greet me and the other new postulants. "Welcome, Barbara," they said, shaking my hand and giving me hugs. "We will pray for your perseverance."

A girl I knew from high school—she was a Holy Names novice now—appeared in the vestibule to greet me and lead me off to the dorm. There, on the wall of the alcove where I would be sleeping, was my postulant's habit—a muslin chemise, a black serge underskirt with big pockets, an ankle-length black serge dress with long sleeves and white cuffs, and a cape. Also a black hair net, black cotton stockings and finally, the black Girl Scout shoes, which my mother and I had sent up ahead of time from home. It all sounds oppressive, but it wasn't. Not in the least. Not for me. I was excited. I was getting ready for the rest of my life. I was only seventeen, but I knew that this was the thing I was supposed to be doing.

While I was getting dressed, my parents were out on the front lawn waiting for me, along with the parents of the other new postulants. One of the sisters, not very graciously, came up to my father and asked him to write the check for my dowry, which is the money held in trust for you in case you ever leave the community. It wasn't that much money, especially when you consider that later on the community paid for my college education and my master's degree. But my parents hadn't been expecting this, and the timing was bad. My father, never one to be tight with money, got emotional.

"I've just given you my daughter," he said. "Isn't that enough?"

By the time we postulants came outdoors again, dressed in the new habits, it was late in the afternoon. Our parents were given only a few minutes to say good-bye before we were whisked off again, this time to the chapel for a ceremony and, following that, to be folded into the routine of the convent—dinner, recreation, night prayer, and at nine o'clock, grand silence and bed.

Once you went behind those convent doors, that was it for your mother and father. During my novitiate, my parents could see me only once a month for an hour or two, then they had to say good-bye and make the long trip back to Southern California. For years after that, all during the fifties and most of the sixties, we didn't go home for visits, not for Thanksgiving, not for Christmas, not for birthdays or anniversaries. I couldn't even go home for my grandfather's funeral. "It's worse than the Marine Corps," my father used to say.

Convent life wasn't easy for me. Right from the beginning I got into trouble. I didn't just accept all those rules and constraints. We were supposed to observe silence, for instance, except at specific times, but if I needed to say something to someone, make a comment or offer a supportive remark, I did.

As a novice, I did a lot of work in the garden. The novice mistress was a hardy person, and she'd have us doing things like putting in sprinkler systems and breaking up cement sidewalks. One time she gave me a task to do, and when I realized it was going to take more than one of us to do it, I asked another novice to get a couple of people and take care of it.

When the novice mistress saw someone else doing the work, she asked me about it. "I delegated authority," I said. Naively, I thought she would see the virtue in this; in high school, we had been encouraged to share and delegate work.

"No. That was not delegating authority," she said. "That was disobedience." The novice mistress wasn't angry. She was firm. This wasn't the first time she'd had to remind me of what convent life was all about—you do what you're told. But I didn't buy it; I was my father's daughter.

The constraints of convent life didn't stop me, though, and seven years after I entered the Sisters of the Holy Names, I made my final vows. I was given a simple gold ring to signify my commitment to God and to this way of life. The ring was made partly from one of my mother's wedding rings, and it was engraved with the letters "JMJ" for the names of Jesus, Mary, and Joseph.

After the ceremony, the novice mistress stopped me in the hallway. "Congratulations," she said. "And good luck." Then she added with a smile, "You're way too independent, you know. You want to question everything. I'll be surprised if you last."

I stayed with the Sisters of the Holy Names for twenty-five years. Our community prayed together every day, we shared silence together, and after dinner we took walks and talked and laughed together. It was a good life. I loved it. It was a teaching community and I taught music, but for me the teaching part was like third on the list after prayer and community. It was clear to me from the very beginning that it wasn't the classroom or the children that had drawn me into the convent, it was the contemplative aspect and the community itself. Those were the values that were important to me, and for many years they were also among the priorities of my community.

Vatican II changed all that. Religious communities around the world were being asked to go back to their roots, and for the Sisters of the Holy Names that meant teaching. Our whole way of life changed, and the two things that had drawn me into religious life, community and communal prayer, became secondary to the ministry of teaching.

Before Vatican II, we never left the convent after dark, unless you were going somewhere in an ambulance. Now, in the sixties and seventies, we were wearing street clothes and going to meetings at night. At noon, you'd head back to the convent for lunch, grab your mail, and sit down to eat. Then after lunch if it wasn't a teaching day everyone would go off to do this or that. We were free now to do things like go to a restaurant on special occasions and have a glass of wine with dinner. We could spend holidays with our families, which was wonderful for my parents and me, but it meant that the sisters had to make elaborate plans if we were to have any kind of time together at Christmas and the other holidays. To me, it felt like living in a hotel.

I kept trying to make all this work. I joined committees and we'd talk ad nauseam about how to recapture some of what we had lost. It finally came to the point where I couldn't talk about it anymore. For me the new shoes just didn't fit.

Meanwhile, a lot of good things were coming out of Vatican II. For one thing, sisters were being invited to train as spiritual directors to give private, one-on-one guidance to individuals who wanted to deepen their relationship with God. Within the Catholic tradition, there had been a small number of women over the centuries who had done this work, but they were the exceptions.

During the late sixties, a Holy Names sister named Sister Mary Xavierita began organizing sisters to be trained as spiritual directors. Spiritual direction was not the mission of the Holy Names Sisters, teaching was, but Sister Xavierita wasn't afraid to be on the cutting edge of something. She asked me if I'd like to give it a try. I said sure, I would. And I loved it right from the beginning. Typically, I'd meet with a person once a month for an hour. We might talk about the person's prayer life, family, or job, but in spiritual direction, the focus is on the directee's relationship with God, so the role of the director is not to give advice, but to listen and ask questions about how the Holy Spirit is moving in their life. It's like eavesdropping.

At that time, there was no training or certification for spiritual direction. It was all so new. We'd have these workshops and talk about what we were doing, but the only way you knew whether you were called to do this work was if anybody came to see you. And people came to see me! Lots of them. Other sisters, but also lay people, whose spirituality was often as deep or deeper than what we as religious women were experiencing.

Soon I was meeting with directees every evening after teaching sixth grade all day. It was exhausting and I didn't think I could keep it up. So I went to the sister who decided where people in my community were sent to teach or work and I told her that either I was going to do spiritual direction or I was going to teach; I couldn't do both, and my preference was to do spiritual ministry. The sister conferred with the community leadership in Los Gatos, and the answer was either take a job as principal of this school that had an opening or go back into the classroom. Spiritual direction was not even mentioned.

I was crushed. I sensed that God was calling me toward a spiritual ministry, but my community wasn't going to let me do it. They had other priorities; they had slots to fill in schools. After meeting with my own spiritual director, I agreed to take the principal's job for a year. But I was terribly sad that my community couldn't see the need that I saw. In desperation, I went to see this Jesuit priest friend of mine who ran a retreat house in Los Angeles. He knew me well and I felt free to speak my mind. We sat in the living room of his retreat house and I talked.

"You know, John," I said finally. "I'm so frustrated I could go out and start my own community."

I wasn't serious, of course. Who was I to start a new religious community? But I was bursting with frustration and this was the most outrageous thing I could think of to say. John, on the other hand, was completely serious. He was a man who listened carefully. He looked at me thoughtfully for a long moment.

"Well," he said at last. "Maybe you need to think about that."

You could have knocked me over with a feather. It was like that moment under the willow tree. I was so shocked I went back to the convent that night and drank two beers. I had never thought of something as radical as starting a new community. It seemed so impossible. But now the seed had been planted, and I thought maybe this is supposed to happen. All around me, I saw the need. On college campuses, students were studying Buddhism and Transcendental Meditation and going off to join the Hare Krishnas and the Moonies. And in the churches, I heard Catholic lay people asking, where do we go to deepen the contemplative aspect of our lives? I was seeing in other people what I was hungering for myself and I felt drawn to do something about it. I felt that God was calling me to create a place, a community where people could go to deepen their prayer lives.

The principal's job was demanding, though not as exhausting as classroom teaching had been, and I had time to draw up a proposal and present it to the provincial administration. My hope was to provide spiritual ministry to the laity in a parish—spiritual direction, retreats, reflection groups. The decision-makers at Holy Names responded by saying that if I was serious, I would need to get a paying job to support myself and the project. With the provincial's permission, I took a job coordinating the religious education program at the Newman Center near the University of

California campus in Berkeley.

I moved into a house with three other sisters who were also taking time away from their communities. All three women shared my vision of a spiritual ministry to the laity. But within a couple of years, two of the sisters had left the project, and in 1981, the remaining sister and I moved into a house in the Glenview district of Oakland. But a few months later she decided to go back to her community. The day she moved out, I cried so hard my face was swollen. Everything was getting whittled away from me—first my Holy Names community and now the sisters I'd thought were going to be my team. I was down to just me. I couldn't pay the rent by myself, and all I had was ideas.

Just when I thought all was lost, several friends—lay people— at the Newman Center who shared my vision came through with some monetary help. That was an important financial turning point for me. The spiritual turning point came later, in December 1982, when I came across John Main's book, *Letters from the Heart.*

John Main was a Benedictine monk from London who had founded a community in Montreal that focused on the teaching and practice of Christian meditation. Anybody and everybody, clergy and lay people, were welcome to join in its life and prayer. What intrigued me was its focus on Christian meditation. Silent meditation was not new to Christianity. It had been practiced in the early church, and now John Main and some others were reviving it.

I wanted to learn more, so the following summer I went to Montreal to spend a month in the monastery. It was like nothing I had ever seen. First, it was in the heart of the city, near McGill University. Students and city people could get to it easily. Also, the resident monks and whoever came to visit—lay people, priests, and religious like me—were all one community, no division between monks and visitors. When we prayed, we prayed together. When we ate, we ate together. When we recreated in the evening, we recreated together. When we meditated, we meditated together—five times a day. The schedule wasn't overly rigid though; one day a week was a free day for everyone.

A week or two into my stay, I realized that this was what I had been looking for. A Christian meditation community that welcomed everybody. A monastery in an urban setting that people could get to easily. This was what was needed back home in Oakland. A place like, but not exactly like, this one here in Montreal. But I had no idea where to start.

That's when I heard that Father Jean LeClercq was coming to the Montreal priory that summer. LeClercq was esteemed by a lot of people as the wisest Benedictine in the world, and for me at that point he was the closest thing to God I could get to. So I asked for a chance to talk to him. I told him I wanted to create something new, but I didn't know what or how.

LeClercq just stroked his little goatee beard and said, "Well, Sister. The way monasteries got started was somebody started them. Just start and see what happens. If God wants it, it will work."

That was the advice he gave me. Just start. I came back to the house on Elston Avenue and turned the basement into a meditation room and a chapel. With some money donated by my mother, I bought chairs and cushions and I carpeted the floors. Then I sent out advertisements to places like the Newman Center announcing Christian meditation and prayer every day of the week.

For the first few months, I was the only one who showed up most of the time. I'd go downstairs to the meditation room, sit on a couple of the cushions and close my eyes. I'd sit there quietly, as

I learned to do in Montreal, and repeat my mantra. (It is *marana-tha*, a word Jesus probably spoke when he prayed, and it means "Come, Lord" in Aramaic.) I was still brand new to Christian meditation. Most everything I knew about it I had learned during those few weeks in Montreal. And, while there had always been people around me during meditation time in Montreal, I was now alone more often than not. I was terrified. Sitting there, all I felt was a nothingness. Not only was it a nothing, it was a negative nothing. I thought I was going crazy. I didn't know if there was anything inside of me.

A lot of what I had learned in the convent, even though it affected me deeply, emphasized the externals—the way you dressed, the way you walked, the way you sang the psalms, the way you interacted at recreation. None of it focused specifically on the internal. My whole life, in fact, had been projected outward. I had done everything in community with other people, first my family, then the Sisters of the Holy Names.

Now, I was feeling such emptiness and depression. I was going through menopause. My mother had passed away in the midst of all this. My father had died several years earlier. I had left my community, my three housemates had moved out, I was living alone, and I was trying to create something new.

I found the experience of meditating so frightening that I had to ask people to go downstairs and be with me while I did it. Of course, God was there the whole time, but I sure didn't have any sense of that. Books on spirituality describe this dark night of the soul experience, but reading about it is not the same thing as going through it. I didn't give up, though, because friends encouraged me, and I had a wonderful spiritual director, another Jesuit priest, who kept saying, "You just have to keep going and trust."

Little by little, the community began to take shape, and I

could leave my job at the Newman Center. I chose the name He-sed Community after *hesed*, the Hebrew word for God's faithful love. One of the first to come was a man who had been practicing Buddhist meditation who was surprised to learn there was such a thing as Christian meditation. As the months went by, more and more people came, mostly lay people, and I found out that what people say is true—meditating in a group is much easier than do-ing it by yourself. And once you've felt that web of support, it's easier to do it by yourself.

Very gradually, over the space of a few years, the meditation experience became a positive for me. Silent meditation, if you let it, changes your daily life for the better. I felt more whole, more complete, more peaceful and less on the defensive. Whether it's Buddhist, Christian, or Transcendental, meditation gives you a sense of yourself that you don't get any other way. If you come at meditation from a Christian point of view, you believe that the spirit of Christ lives in you, as the scriptures say, and you believe that Spirit is transforming you from within.

Sitting in silence is a prayer of faith. You totally let go of be-ing in charge, which is different from what most prayer is about, because as long as we use words, we are in control. Most of us as Christians have been taught that prayer is talking to God. We feel the responsibility to do something, to be active when we pray, but in meditation, you enter it with the idea that you will let the Spirit transform you. You don't talk, you listen.

I prefer silent meditation to verbal prayer now, because I like to think of prayer as the process of opening up to what already exists, which is the presence of God within us. To me God is a presence. God doesn't have a form. I don't think of God as Fa-ther or Mother. God is present in everyone and everything, and my awareness of that is heightened as I meditate and open up to

God. I love the word *marinate*. To me, meditation is marinating in God.

The leadership of the Sisters of the Holy Names was very patient with me during this time. They were interested in and supportive of what I was trying to do. But it was becoming clear to them that Hesed, as it was evolving, did not fit into the mission of the Holy Names community. As a sister of the Holy Names, I was a teaching sister, not a monk or a cloistered nun—and what I was doing at Hesed was clearly monastic. It was time, they said, to make a decision. I could continue on at Hesed or I could come back to the community.

I was devastated. The Sisters of the Holy Names had been my life for thirty years, from eighth grade through high school, and on through my novitiate and my adult life as a sister. The sisters were my family, my home. Leaving them would be like getting a divorce.

But the new calling was persistent. Early in 1984, at the direction of my superiors, I wrote a letter to Rome requesting a dispensation from my vows as a Holy Names sister, and a few months later my request was granted. When I met with the provincial to sign the papers, she gave me copies of the documents and kept some for herself. And that was that. The whole thing took ten minutes. I had been in the community for more than twenty-five years and that was the send-off I got. A handful of documents. A little later, a small check arrived in the mail. It was my dowry.

Later that year, I took vows as a Benedictine. Technically, I'm a monastic now, not a sister or a nun, though people still call me Sister Barbara. I don't wear a nun's habit or a monk's robes. I dress like everyone else, most days in a shirt, slacks, and tennies. I enjoy that. I like to pop people's balloons about what a sister looks like and acts like.

Hesed has been more fruitful than I ever dreamed. It's almost completely supported by our members and the people who come and join us for prayer. As far as I know, there is nothing quite like Hesed anywhere else—an urban, non-resident, Benedictine community where the teaching and practice of Christian meditation are the priority. There is no community of monks in residence at Hesed, which means that our members—most of whom have jobs and families and homes—don't have to feel they are just an adjunct to the "real" Hesed. They are Hesed.

We don't sponsor a soup kitchen; we don't do peace and justice work or anything like that. Most of our members are already doing those things elsewhere in their lives. We try to provide a spiritual foundation for them with prayer, silent meditation, retreats—and community. A woman who has been meditating at Hesed for years once made the comment, "We may not know a lot about each other, but we know each other." That's the fruit of a regular practice of sitting together in silence.

I have never wanted to be anything but a sister, from that moment under the willow tree until now, all these years later. The desire to devote my life to God has never left me. It's been like cement. It has persevered. I still wear the gold ring that was given to me when I first professed my vows. The letters JMJ wore off long ago, and I've had them replaced with the word Hesed, but it's the same ring and the same commitment—my ongoing relationship with God. As for the Sisters of the Holy Names, I continue to be grateful to them for what they have given me and for all the friendships I continue to enjoy.

Just before my father died in the late seventies he asked my mother and me to meet with him and Sister Emily Marie at Los Gatos. I had no idea what he was going to say. It turned out he wanted to set up a small trust fund to provide for my retirement, just in case I ever wanted to leave the Sisters of the Holy Names. I told him not to bother, I would never need it. He went ahead and set it up anyway, and a week later he died. Within a few years, I was writing my letter to Rome. It's been years now since my father put that money away for me, but I can still feel him smiling. And this time the joke is on me.

PART FOUR: *God's Problem—*
Human Suffering

8

Yes, God Is Good

Sister Barbara Hazzard, Mark Zapalik, Orenzia Bernstine—all three have great faith in a provident universe. All three were able to give their lives over to God. The widowed Mark Zapalik goes so far as to trust that God will choose a suitable mate for him. For Barbara, Mark, and Orenzia, God is unfailingly good.

But I wonder, is their confidence misplaced? Do human beings matter? Does God intervene in human life? Is the ultimate reality the compassionate, all-knowing, all-powerful God of Christianity, Judaism, and Islam? Or something else entirely? Is it trustworthy? I'd like to know.

Years ago, when I was eight-and-a-half months pregnant with my daughter Christina, now thirty-one, I was sitting beside a shallow swimming pool noisy with babies and toddlers when I realized with a start that my baby wasn't moving. I hadn't felt her move all that day or the night before. Was she dead?

I slipped on my sandals, got in my car, and headed home. As I steered my old red Fiat down our hill, my thoughts turned to God. I could ask God to save my baby. I could ask for a miracle. But God doesn't do miracles these days, as far as I knew. And I refused to beg. If God was cruel enough to take away babies and spare them on a whim, I wanted nothing to do with him. I hated him.

My doctor ordered an ultrasound test. The transducer felt like a dentist's drill on my belly. I didn't like it and neither apparently did Christina. As soon as she felt its vibrations, she began rolling and punching at my insides. My baby was alive. But I couldn't bring myself to thank God for my daughter's life any more than I had been able to ask for it earlier. How could I thank God for something God had so nearly taken away from me, and so gratuitously? God—and if there was no God, then the universe I was born into—was not to be trusted.

Now, years later, I still wonder, do we live in a friendly universe? Or is it indifferent, insensate—hostile even? How do we explain human suffering and pain? We are born, we experience disappointment after disappointment and loss after loss. Our loved ones die, we die. Some of us live comfortable lives between birth and death, but most of us live lives of illness, poverty, violence, or all of the above. Can such suffering possibly be consistent with an intentional, compassionate universe?

The answer has to be no. Or so it seemed to me until I talked the question over with Robert Tharratt, Elizabeth Felts, and Cerridwen Fallingstar.

Robert Tharratt has suffered much. His B-17 airplane was shot down over Germany during World War II. He was captured, imprisoned, and forced on a brutal five-hundred-mile winter march across Germany. And yet Robert believes that God is good, God cares, God is trustworthy. And he has the story to prove it.

I located Robert through a local Veteran's Center. When I phoned him he invited me to come to the condominium he shared with his wife Jeane in a grassy suburb not far from my old *Contra Costa Times* office. Robert had converted one of the condominium's upstairs bedrooms into a home office. One wall was decorated with military photos. Another was covered with military weaponry, including a Hitler Youth knife inscribed with the words Blut und Ehre, "blood and honor."

A soft-spoken man with blue eyes and a dimpled chin, Robert had retired from his job as a building supplies salesman, and now he was taking time to put together a thick booklet describing his wartime experiences. Included was a copy of a telegram addressed to his mother:

"THE SECRETARY OF WAR DESIRES ME TO EXPRESS HIS DEEP REGRET THAT YOUR SON STAFF SERGEANT ROBERT THARRATT HAS BEEN REPORTED MISSING IN ACTION SINCE TEN SEPTEMBER OVER GERMANY."

Robert's story begins in the ball turret of a B-17 bomber.

Robert Tharratt—His Story

We were bombing Nuremberg on the day our plane was shot down. It was noon on a clear day, September 10, 1944. I was twenty-one years old and it was my eighteenth mission. From where we were, at thirty thousand feet, I couldn't see people. All I knew was we were bombing factories and industrial targets. Were there people in those buildings? I didn't know. I had no feeling about that. We were just doing a job as far as I was concerned.

Our target was a synthetic oil manufacturing plant outside Nuremberg. We had dropped our bombs and we were pulling off the target when three bursts of flack exploded around us. Right away, our number four engine caught shrapnel and started to fail. Two more bursts of flack exploded. Our number one engine went out, and number two caught fire. Three of our four engines were down.

Billy Lowry, our top gunner, called out over the radio. "I've been hit."

I was ball turret gunner, and Lowry's position was directly behind the pilot and copilot, a distance from me probably of twenty-five to thirty feet. I knew everybody up front was busy trying to control the airplane, so I radioed the crew that I was going to Lowry's aid. I opened the ball turret hatch, climbed out, picked up a walk-around oxygen bottle, and made my way forward through the radio room and the bomb bay toward the top turret.

The pilots were working overtime to control the plane. They had trimmed it and gotten it into automatic pilot, and now the plane was in a controlled downward glide. Our plane was losing altitude steadily. One engine was not going to keep us in the air for long. And if the fire in number two reached any of our gas tanks, the tank would explode and we wouldn't be going anywhere but down.

I was part of a ten-man Army Air Force crew flying missions over Germany from England with the 96th Bomb Group, 338th Squadron, Eighth Air Force. Our B-17 was originally designed in 1935, and it was the old workhorse bomber of World War II. They called it the Flying Fortress because it was built so rugged and had so many guns—two in the nose turret, two in the top turret where Billy was, one in the radio room, two in the ball turret where I was, two on either side of the waist, and two in the tail. Altogether, our plane had thirteen fifty-caliber machine guns protecting it.

I had been trained as a flight engineer, but since I was the smallest person in our crew I was assigned to the ball turret. I was upset about this, but I didn't want to make a fuss with my crew, so I didn't say anything. The ball turret is shaped like a half ball about four and a half feet across. It hangs out the bottom of the plane's fuselage. The ball turret gunner steps down into the turret from the airplane and sits curled up on a little armor plate, feet pushed up against one side of the turret, head and shoulders flat against the other. You had two guns and you could aim them by moving the turret any way you wanted. Back and forth. Up and down. All the way around, nearly three-hundred-sixty degrees.

I was small, but I wasn't really small enough for the ball turret. Five feet seven and a half inches, one hundred fifty-five pounds. A smaller person could take his parachute in with him, and if anything happened, he could reach down, open the hatch and fall out. But I was too big to carry my chute in there. I had to leave it outside the turret. If the airplane got into trouble and I didn't have time to get to my parachute, that ball turret would be my coffin.

That's why the pilot assigned one of the waist gunners, Henry DiRocco, to check on me. DiRocco was supposed to see that I was okay in the ball turret and to get me out of there if there was a problem.

Those old planes weren't pressurized, you see. There was no heat, no oxygen. Just the metal skin of the airplane between you and the elements. The air was pretty thin at thirty thousand feet, so we all used oxygen tanks. I can still smell the rubber of those masks. And it could get cold, fifty below zero. Winter, summer, it didn't matter. It was like flying in a tin can up there. We wore fleece-lined suits and helmets to keep warm, and when we went aboard we took off our GI shoes and put on these sheepskin flying boots, fleece on the inside, leather on the outside.

If the mission took eight hours, I'd be curled up in that ball turret approximately six hours with no chance to stretch my legs. On a ten-hour mission, it might be eight hours. Every once in a while, DiRocco would call out over the radio, checking to make sure my oxygen was working.

"How you doing, Bob?"

"I'm fine."

"Yeah?"

"Yeah."

I wasn't really fine. I was scared all the time. I was claustrophobic in that ball turret, my knees just inches from my chin. It took an awful lot to stay put in that small space. I prayed a lot, "Oh, good Lord, look after me." Well, maybe I used stronger language. But the faith was always there. It had to be, otherwise, I couldn't do my job.

When I got to Lowry, he was stuck in the top turret. He had been hit in the elbow with shrapnel. His right arm was bleeding and useless and he couldn't get himself out of there. I had to unhook him—straps, radio, oxygen—and pull him out. I was just getting him out of the turret when the bail-out bell rang. That bail-out bell means business: get out of the airplane, now. No time to do a goddamn thing but get out of this airplane.

Lowry had his parachute on, but he couldn't fasten the harness. I started to fasten it for him, but I saw there was no way he going to pull that ripcord with his right hand. I turned his parachute around and hooked it up backward, so when the time came, Lowry could use his left hand to pull the cord.

The wound looked like it needed a tourniquet, but the pilot was shouting, "Everybody out! Out!" No time to go to the radio room for first aid. I motioned Lowry toward the nose hatch. I sat him down, and he put his legs out the door. "Billy, this is all I can do for you," I said and I pushed him out the hatch.

I hoped Lowry wouldn't bleed to death before he hit ground. I also hoped that once he hit ground, someone would get him to the hospital or put a tourniquet on him. It seemed like a lot to hope for.

Lowry's situation was under control, but there I was, twenty thousand feet over enemy territory, and my plane was going down fast. It could go out of control at any moment. If it went into a tailspin, I would be pressed against the skin, and I wouldn't be able to move—like those carnival rides where the floor drops out from under you, and you're stuck against the wall. If that happened, I wouldn't be able to escape the plane, let alone get to my parachute, which was still back there next to the ball turret.

We were younger and thinner and faster in those days. We could run from the front of the plane to the back in a matter of seconds. It was a tight fit though. Our B-17 could carry two ton of bomb, and the bomb racks came right up to the catwalk, so the catwalk was narrow, maybe eight inches wide, where it passed through the bomb bay. We had to turn our shoulders sideways to fit through.

The bail-out bell was still ringing. I ran through the bomb bay and found my parachute next to the ball turret, with my boots. I didn't bother with the boots. I grabbed my chute and looked toward the cockpit. The pilot was getting out of his seat, waving his hand and motioning, "Go! Go! Go!"

The radio operator had bailed out, the tail gunner was gone, and the pilot was getting ready to go out the nose hatch. DiRocco was waiting for me at the waist hatch. He wouldn't bail until he was sure I was okay. "Come on! Come on!" he waved.

I strapped my parachute on and stepped up to the waist hatch. Standing there, I realized I still had my forty-five caliber gun on me. I didn't want to hit the ground carrying a loaded forty-five; I figured if I came down with a gun, they'd shoot me first and ask questions later. I took it out of my shoulder holster and threw it back into the plane. DiRocco did the same.

DiRocco jumped, which left me standing by myself at the opening of the waist hatch. Up till now my thoughts had been rushed: Help Lowry! Get him out of the plane! Get your chute and get the hell out of here! But now, standing at the waist hatch, looking out, there was nothing but blue sky in front of me. My mind slowed down. I thought, well, you're in God's hands now. And, phhht, out the door I went.

I was born in England on May 17, 1923. My parents were English. My father was an aeronautical engineer; consequently we went wherever the airplanes were being built. Montreal. Baltimore. And finally Reseda, California, which is where I went to high school. With all our moves, the actual going to church was spotty. But my sisters and I learned our prayers, and my father was proud to say, "In all my years, I have never gone to bed without kneeling and saying my prayers. I did it in World War I, and I'll probably do it when I am on my death bed." So for me, yes, there was a God. He wouldn't let me get hurt. And every time I did something stupid and fell on my face, I figured, God's going to pick me up. He'll look after me no matter what.

My father had fought in World War I, and my mother's uncle had died in a German prison camp during that war. They had him working in a salt mine. So my mother had some pretty strong feelings about the Bosche, as she called them. Despite all that, I wasn't brought up to hate the Germans. Even when I was overseas, flying those bombing missions, I didn't hate Germans.

I had no fear when I jumped out of the waist hatch. I didn't open my chute right away. They tell you in training to wait until you are close enough to the ground to distinguish between a cow and a horse. The enemy would be shooting at you from the ground, and if you opened your parachute too soon, you'd be an easy target. If you waited, you'd be moving too fast for anyone to get a bead on you. So I waited.

I fell eighteen thousand feet without opening my parachute. I fell bodily from something like twenty thousand feet to two thousand feet with absolutely no fear, knowing God was with me. I felt he just took me in his hands and floated me down.

It was so quiet. There was nothing around me but air. The sound of the airplane engines was gone. I had on my fleece-lined helmet, so there was no whistling of air past my head. My clothes weren't sticking out; nothing was flapping. I was moving at maybe a hundred-and-twenty miles an hour, but the earth wasn't rushing up at me. Nothing was. Even the nearest clouds were way off on the horizon, not moving. If I moved a hand or an arm, it sent me off in a different direction, so I just sat there with my arms folded, moving my head a little to look around. It was like sitting on a rocking chair. It was up to God, what was going to happen, and I had enough faith to accept that that's the way it was.

Floating and looking down, I saw that I was in farm country. I saw a plowed field and, off in the distance, a little woods. I tried to pick out houses and churches. I was thinking, when do I pull the ripcord? And pretty soon . . . there was a horse . . . and there was a cow. Just like they said it would be. I pulled the ripcord.

I didn't try to pull any risers. I just hung on. I landed feet first. When my feet dug into the ground, the wind grabbed the chute. It pulled me over and drugged me a little way until I could disconnect it. The chute deflated. I rolled it up and hid it in a pile of manure waiting to be spread on the field. Then I headed for the woods.

I didn't have a chance. As soon as I started out toward the woods, I heard voices behind me. Boys' voices. Boisterous, teenaged voices, screaming and yelling. I turned to look. It was the Hitler Youth, come to get me. There were about a dozen of them, rage in their faces, spitting and growling. I thought they might kill me. I put my hands in the air and surrendered.

The boys all wore shorts. Some had on those *Lederhosen*, the leather shorts with leather suspenders that German boys wear. They all had short hair, blond to light brunette. Nice-looking individuals. I was only a few years older than those boys and I had the same light brown hair, light skin, and narrow face and nose. We didn't look all that different, but I was the enemy coming down in their territory. I had just finished bombing their city. And if it was left up to them, it was my butt they would kick.

Two soldiers had the group under control, fortunately for me. They told the boys to go this way and that way. Pretty soon, they had me surrounded. A couple of the boys shook their fists at me. Some took out their Hitler Youth knives and waved them at me. The soldiers told the boys to put the knives away. They saw my empty holster, and one of them frisked me all over. Then he pointed me in a direction and said something in German. I started walking. The boys went ahead, chatting, hopping, skipping and jumping. Just having a ball. The soldiers and I brought up the rear. It was kind of slow going because I was still wearing my fleece flying boots. After about a quarter mile, we came to the Hitler Youth camp.

DiRocco was there. He had been picked up a quarter mile in the other direction. The Hitler Youth lined up in front of the flagpole, and the commandant ranted Hitler this and Hitler that. DiRocco and I stood on either side of the pole, dejected. We were in a heap of hurt. I looked up. There was a cross-arm on the flagpole with two ropes hanging from it, one on each side. One was over my head, the other was over DiRocco's.

"DiRocco," I said. "They're going to hang us."

"Aw. They wouldn't hang us."

"Look up."

DiRocco looked up. "Oh, shit."

The commandant kept on going with his *Heil Hitlers*. DiRocco was Italian, from Long Island. He had grown up with Italians and Germans and Poles, and he had a smattering of all the languages.

"What's he saying?" I said.

"He's saying we're *Fliegergangster*, murderers of women and children."

The commandant finished his harangue, and the soldiers marched us out of the camp and across the fields to a small town that I don't know the name of. DiRocco had had time to put on his GI boots before he bailed out of the plane, so he was okay. But I kept falling behind, shuffling through the field in my flying boots.

"Mach schnell!" the soldier shouted at me. "Hurry up!" I couldn't go any faster. The soldier whacked me square in the back with the butt of his rifle.

In town, DiRocco and I were put in a truck with everyone else in our crew. Billy Lowry was the only one missing. The truck stopped at a hospital to pick him up, but the doctors wouldn't release him because of his wounds, so our truck headed on toward Nuremberg without him. For me, the war was over. My eighteenth mission would never be completed. I was a prisoner of war, a *Kriegsgefangener*. No telling what was going to happen from here on in.

We were taken to Stalagluft IV, a prison camp up on the Baltic near Gdansk, in what is now Polish territory. Our B-17 crew was broken up and separated, but as soon as I arrived I got to talking with these two fellas, Arthur Dean Batchelor of Glendale, California, and Louis Palermo of Los Angeles. We had a lot in common. We were all from Southern California, and we had all messed around with restoring and hopping up old cars in our high school days.

The three of us could talk about cars by the hour. We'd sit there on the floor of the barracks, talking about what kind of a hot rod we'd build if we had the facilities. We did everything by memory, digging in our minds for the names of parts and manufacturers we'd heard about before we went into the service. We thought about the engine block, and usually we wanted to build a Ford V8. Then we'd talk about what kind of heads, drive shaft, cam shaft, and crank we'd put on that V8. We'd decide on the carburetion, a Holley carburetor probably. All high performance parts. Mag wheels. Hydraulic brakes. We didn't put anything down on paper, we built it all mentally.

There wasn't much to eat at Stalagluft IV. Potatoes, kohlrabi soup, cabbage soup, black bread, and ersatz coffee made with acorns. That was the diet. We were too hungry to exercise much, so we talked about cars and that kept us from going crazy. That's how we got to be buddies. Art, Lou, and I. We looked after each other, we shared our Red Cross packages, everything. We were a combine.

A dislike for Germans built up in me at Stalagluft IV because of the way they treated us. We didn't get enough food. We were kicked and hit. We'd see the guards smoking Lucky Strike and Camel cigarettes that they'd stolen from our Red Cross packages—they'd flash them in front of us so we'd know they had American cigarettes and we didn't. Things like that.

One of the Germans in particular liked to hit the prisoners. We called him Big Stoop. He'd cup his hand and hit a fella on the side of the head, causing a lot of pain and sometimes a broken eardrum. Fortunately, that one never happened to me. But another time, after we'd been strip-searched, I put my foot up on a stool to tie my shoe, and Big Stoop gave me a boot. Kicked me clear across the room, because he didn't think I should put my foot on the stool.

When you're treated decently, there's no animosity. But if you're hit with rifle butts and kicked and swore at and threatened to be shot and killed for every day that you're in captivity, I don't care who you are, you build up a dislike and a hatred for certain people.

In January 1945, the Allied Forces—the Soviets, the British, and the Americans—were closing in on Germany. Soviet troops had entered Warsaw, just two hundred miles from our prison camp. There were a lot of us in the camp, including thousands of Americans. The Germans planned to use us as a bargaining chip if they had to surrender. To keep us from falling into the hands of the Allies, they were moving us back into Germany.

The night of February 4, 1945, our guards told us to get ready to move. We all made packs to carry our belongings. To make a pack in prison camp meant you had to use your ingenuity. You took a towel or a shirt, sewed up the edges and made a bag. Then you hooked up a couple of socks or the sleeves of the shirt and made straps that came over your shoulders, so you had sort of a backpack. Inside the pack you could have a change of socks or an extra pair of underwear and whatever bits of food or bread you had. Your blanket you rolled up and put over the top and tied it on. That was your pack. It might weigh fifteen pounds total, which for us was heavy.

The next morning, they moved the whole camp. They put the sick and those who couldn't move into boxcars and moved them west, about three thousand men. The rest of us, around six thousand American and British airmen, went on the road. We marched. My combine, Art, Lou, and I, went out the gate with a group of approximately three thousand men. Later we broke up into units of five hundred or so, each unit taking a different route.

They marched us from Gdansk toward Berlin, then around the north side of Berlin and south toward Leipzig. We used all back roads through farm areas; they didn't want us near the cities. Art kept a daily log on little pieces of scratch paper with all the places we spent the night. Places you've never heard of. Griesfelden. Kirkwitz. Wollin. Medow. Zieslubbe. Heidorf.

The guards didn't seem to know where we were going from one day to the next. One day we went seven kilometers and there was no place to stay, so we turned around and went back to where we were the night before. We were like so many cattle being herded down the road and every once in a while given something to eat. We'd sleep in the woods or in open fields on the wet ground, wherever the guards could find space for us. If there were barns, they stuffed us into barns.

The winter of 1944-1945 was the worst Germany had seen since the turn of the century. Freezing weather. Rain. Snow. Ice. We weren't dressed for the cold and we were wet most of the time. I had a GI overcoat and shirt, a knit cap and blue wool Royal Air Force pants, all from the Red Cross. And I was lucky: I had been given GI boots to replace my fleece flying boots a week after I was captured. My boots were wet all the time, but they were leather, and they didn't have holes in them. Other fellas had partials—sandals—or their shoes wore out on the march. Some wrapped their feet in blankets.

On the march, you laid down in your clothes at night and you got up in your clothes in the morning. As soon as you got up, you were ready to march. They handed you a piece of black bread, and you held out your canteen and they gave you some ersatz coffee. Then we were ready to move. That's the way we lived. Starving and cold. To this day I suffer from—most of the fellas on that march suffer from—frostbitten toes and fingers. According to the VA, I've lost twenty percent of the feeling in my fingers. I have to be careful when I reach for something hot. Most of us have back problems, arthritis, from sleeping on the cold ground and being wet so much of the time.

Most of us had diarrhea and we were relieving ourselves at the side of the road. Sometimes we did that as we marched through a town. We had to. Couldn't help it. And here you were, bloody feces coming out of your body, and some German comes over and gives you a kick because you're doing it in their streets. But what else could we do? We were miserable. We were filthy. We hadn't washed our clothes or had a bath outside of bathing in muddy water for months.

Some of the guys tried to escape, but they came back. The German people weren't going to give you anything, outside of killing you. They didn't have food either, and they thought it was all our fault, we were the enemy. A lot of fellas ended up being killed by civilians. Better to stay on the march. If you were going to get a potato, anything, it would be as a prisoner with the group.

We lost people from the cold. Frozen. We lost people from just giving up. We lost people because they had bad feet. Blisters went to sores. Sores went to gangrene and that was it. Sometimes prisoners were left by the side of the road. Sometimes we heard they were shot. Of the six thousand men who started out from Stalagluft IV, as many as fifteen hundred died or were unaccounted for.

When you get into situations like that, you have a tendency to blame God. If we had a miserable day, who did we blame? The good Lord. The next day, if the sun was shining and we could maybe get a potato, it was, "God, you're forgiven. I'm sorry about what I said yesterday."

There were plenty of miserable days, and I have to be truthful, I damned God many a time. "Damn. Damn. Damn," I'd yell. "Damn you, God. You're no better than the Germans. Goddamn you!"

Then somebody would say, "Oh, come on. It's not all that bad. We're still alive."

"Are we? This isn't living, you sonofabitch."

Sometimes one of us would give up and sit down by the edge of the road. When one of us, Art, Lou, or I, became despondent and ready to give up, the other two would take over. We'd grab the fella's pack and throw it over one shoulder, get him in between us, and sort of carry him along. Then somewhere down the line, another one would give up.

Art and Lou tell me—I don't remember this—that at one point I lay down on the ground in the snow and the mud.

"I can't go any farther," I said. "I'm tired. I'm cold. My feet hurt. I can't move."

"Come on, Bob. Let's go."

"No. Let me alone. Let me die right here."

So Art and Lou grabbed my pack and walked away. Now, your pack was all you had. It had everything you owned in it, dry socks, food, canteen. You couldn't make it without your pack.

"You sonsabitches," I yelled after them. "Goddamn you. Come back here. Give me my pack."

But they wouldn't come back. I had to get up off the ground and go staggering after them. That's how they did it, that's how they kept me going. They knew I wouldn't stay there without my pack. Art and Lou were my saviors. If they had left me behind, no telling what would have happened to me. A lot of guys didn't make it because they didn't have help from someone else. And Art and Lou and I—if it hadn't been for each other, we wouldn't have made it.

Another time, Art had dysentery so bad he wanted to give up. "I can't keep going," he said. "I have to stop."

"You're going."

"No. Get the hell away from me."

Lou and I weren't going to leave him behind. We pulled a towel from Art's backpack and diapered him. It was difficult doing this to a person who is twenty-one, twenty-two years old. Later, taking that diaper off, washing it out in a puddle of water, and then looking after a person that way . . . we were all so young . . . It's difficult talking about this. Let me get a tissue. Sorry about that. For years I couldn't cry. I couldn't even think about it. But now the tears come pretty fast.

I came close to losing all faith on that march. I thought I wasn't going to make it. I thought I'd never see my mother and father and sisters ever again. If I didn't die of starvation, the guards would shoot me. They threatened to every day. I got to the point where I lost hope. I lost faith. I didn't care anymore.

I prayed for help. I said to God, "Now is the time. Help me. Get me out of here." But God didn't help. I was on my own. Lou was on his own. Art was on his own. It was up to the three of us. If we were going to get out of this in any way, shape, or form, we had to look after each other, because God sure as hell wasn't.

We spent the night of April 24 in a warehouse not too far from Leipzig. The next day, we heard through the grapevine that the Americans were just a few miles away on the other side of the Elbe River. They were waiting there for the Russians to come in from the east. We could hear the Russians' guns, so we knew it was only a matter of days. The man we called our "man of confidence" went to the German commandant and told him that tomorrow morning we were going over to the American lines.

The commandant said, *"Nein."*

The man of confidence said, "Hey, we haven't had anything to eat for three days. The Russians are coming. There is no sense in putting us in the middle of it. The war will be over soon."

"Nein. Nein. Nein."

The next morning we got up and, not knowing what the Germans would do, we formed up just like we always did and started toward the American lines. Our guards fell in alongside us, the same as they had for eighty-five days. Pretty soon the line came to a stop. Art, Lou, and I weren't near the front, so we didn't know what was happening until word was passed back from the front of the line that an American jeep with an officer and a sergeant had driven up to see what the heck this big bunch of guys coming down the road was.

We began walking again. Then word came back to us that we had reached a river. The Americans were just the other side, and we were going to cross. The bridge to the town of Bitterfeld had been blown up. The Americans had built a catwalk on top of the debris. We were going to use the catwalk to cross.

Our German guards fell back behind us. We were going one way, they were going the other. One guard that I particularly hated passed by me. He had hit me several times along the way, and every time I saw him during the march I thought, "You sonofabitch. You better not be around when I get through with this, because I'm going to kill you." That thought had kept me going for days. I was going to stay alive just so I could kill the sonbitch. But now that I was about to be liberated and this guard was just a few feet away from me, I thought, screw it, why bother?

We prisoners crossed the river, single file. Once we were across, our guards threw their rifles and guns in a pile, crossed the river, and became the prisoners of the Americans. We had marched six hundred miles in eighty-five days, but our actual liberation was anti-climactic. We were free, and that was all you could say about it. I was so down and so beat, no matter what somebody gave me or did for me, I just accepted it, "Gee, thanks," without enthusiasm. I was a zombie.

As we came off the catwalk, the American troops handed each

of us a box of K-rations. Worst thing in the world they could have done. We hadn't had anything to eat in three days, and like fools we ate this concentrated food. Talk about sick! Every one of us. It caused diarrhea you would not believe. We lost a few more men that way.

The next morning, they put us on trucks and took us to a hospital in Halle. The first thing they did at the hospital was make us take off all our clothes. We stripped down to nothing. A few things like the little pieces of paper Art had kept his log on, we were able to save. Everything else, they didn't care, it went into a big bonfire in the courtyard in front of the hospital. Coats, underwear, backpacks, my G.I. boots, everything went into the fire.

We were filthy and full of bugs—lice, fleas, everything. The seams of our clothes, this is where the fleas hid and laid their eggs and kept warm. I hate to say it, but every once in a while on the march, you looked at somebody and you saw the eyebrows moving. It was lice. The underpants I had on, there was no crotch. To keep the bug population down, we would dry shave under the arms and in the crotch, and so consequently just the rubbing of the legs had worn out the crotch of the underwear, and I just had this stuff hanging down in front.

After we'd thrown everything into the bonfire, they came along with powdered DDT and sprayed us. The head. Under the arms. In the crotch. "Bend over." Everywhere. "Close your eyes. Hold your nose. Don't breathe." When they were done with the DDT, we went indoors and got showers, clean undershorts, and a hospital gown. Three days later they weighed me. I weighed a hundred and nine pounds.

After two weeks, we were allowed to go outdoors and walk around. A river ran through the middle of town. Art, Lou, and I decided to go across and get a look at downtown Halle. We stood on a small pier with other people, waiting for a rowboat to shut-tle us across. We had just finished lunch and I was carrying an orange. A German boy about fourteen years old came up to me, pointed at my orange, and said, *"Bitte."* He wanted me to give him my orange. He wasn't being pushy or anything, he just wanted the orange.

He didn't have the Hitler Youth shirt on, but he was wearing *Lederhosen*. I recognized the britches, they were strictly Hitler Youth, and everything came back to me. The starvation, the death threats, the Hitler Youth waving their knives at me.

"Nichts," I told him. *"Raus!"*

The people on the pier looked at me like, "He's just a kid. Give him the orange." The boy kept pestering me.

"Raus!" I said. "Get out of here!"

The boy still wouldn't leave me alone, so I pushed him out of my way, and he fell in the river. Everybody on the pier started jab-bering off at me in German. I couldn't understand what they were saying and I didn't care.

I looked right at them. *"Kriegsgefangener!"* I screamed. "Pris-oner of war! *Kriegsgefangener!"*

They shut up and backed away. One of the men reached down to the boy and pulled him up on the pier. The boy ran off, soaking wet. When the rowboat arrived, Lou, Art, and I climbed in. There was plenty of room in the boat for more people, but nobody else got in. Nobody wanted to cross the river with me.

Our next stop was Camp Lucky Strike at Le Havre, France, where we waited several weeks for transportation home. They fat-tened us up with eggnogs twice a day and liver every other day. Some American airmen from Stalagluft IV showed up while we were there. They said Big Stoop, the soldier who had kicked me across the room, had been one of their guards on the march. Their group had been liberated by Russian troops, and the Russian soldiers had asked the Americans which of the guards had treated them badly. The prisoners pointed at Big Stoop. The Russians tied Big Stoop to the back of a jeep and dragged him around behind it until he was dead.

I can't remember having any feelings about that outside of, "Okay. They got even with the sonofabitch."

My family met me at the Burbank train station. It was the end of June 1945, and I had a thirty-day furlough in my hand. I was wearing a new Class A uniform issued to me at Camp Beale, California. The Army Air Force had arranged for a couple dozen seamstresses to be there to shorten our pants, take a tuck here and a tuck there, and sew on all our ranks and insignias and this, that, and the other thing. The Air Force wanted us to look sharp when we came home, and I guess I did. I had put on about thirty-five pounds since my liberation, and you couldn't tell by looking at me what I had been through.

Everybody was there when I got off the train. My mother and father. My sisters and their husbands that were not away at war. Friends. It was a great homecoming. Hugging and kissing. Everybody was dressed up like it was Sunday church. The men in suits. My brother-in-law in his uniform. The women in dresses and stockings. My mother gussied up with her fur around her neck and one of her pork pie hats on her head. They looked like millionaires. Coming home was the greatest thing in the world. I was safe and free and easy. There was no more reason to be scared.

My mother and father had a big house on three and a half acres in the San Fernando Valley, and they threw me a big, big party. Two young ladies who had worked at my father's office during the war were there. One took a look at me and said, "Why, you don't look like you went through very much."

Maybe she meant it as a compliment, but I was insulted. I said, "You should have seen me two months ago, before they fattened me up."

I didn't want to talk about the war with that girl. I didn't want to talk about it with anyone, not even my family. My father tried. He had been in France during World War I, in the trenches. He'd had a breakdown due to battle fatigue and he knew what was going on in my head. He asked me a few questions. I just kind of shrugged, so he left it at that.

I asked my younger sister about different fellas I had been to high school with. I wanted to contact them. She told me that most of them hadn't come back. When I heard that, I sort of tucked into myself. When the V-J Day celebration for the surrender of Japan came along, I didn't join in the hoopla. To me, there was no one to celebrate with.

In those days, they didn't know about post-traumatic stress. When I reported to Santa Monica in October for separation from the Air Force, they didn't even give me a physical. All this time, from my liberation in April to my discharge in October—including while I was in the hospital in Halle—they never gave me a full physical. They looked us over and asked how we felt, and we'd say, "Great." After what we had been through, we thought we felt fine.

Just before my discharge at Santa Monica, one of the doctors said, "Well, if you have any complaints, now is the time to say so."

"No. I feel fine."

"You sure you don't want to fill out a form, just in case, for the Veterans Administration? Anything that hurts or went wrong? Did you injure yourself?"

"Well, when I parachuted out, I twisted my left knee."

"Okay. We'll put down injured left knee. Anything else?"

"No. Everything's fine."

Then, boom. They called us all into an auditorium. An officer got up in front.

"Well," he said. "You fellas are going out into civilian life. The government thanks you for doing your job. You've seen a lot. You've gone through a lot, and when you get out there, people are not going to understand. Half the things you try to tell them they're not going to believe. So go home and forget the whole thing. Put it out of your mind."

So, okay. We got our discharges and we went on our way. Lou and Art and I saw each other a few more times in 1945 and '46, but pretty soon, we lost touch. We were supposed to put everything out of our minds, and that's what I tried to do.

When I did think back on my time in Germany, I saw everything in black and white. There were no colors in my memory. The sky wasn't blue, the fields weren't green, the tree trunks weren't brown. Everything was black or white. The German people, it didn't matter who they were, they were no good. The only good German was a dead German. That was it. Black and white.

I didn't talk about the war. Even with my father, I didn't share that much. I'd have nightmares and he'd come rushing into the room and throw himself on top of me. "Get hold of yourself, lad. You're dreaming. It's all over." I'd come to, and the first thing he'd do was give me a shot of whiskey.

When I look back on it, even when we were flying in combat, when we'd come back from a mission the first thing they'd do was give us a shot of whiskey and say, "Here. This will calm your nerves." Consequently, every time I had one of these flashbacks, I'd reach for a drink to settle my nerves. This became standard procedure. The Army did it. My father did it. It must be the thing to do. It became a habit. If something cropped up, a normal problem, I covered it with a drink.

For years, I had nightmares. Nightmares of being hungry and not knowing whether I would survive. Nightmares of watching a plane, a crew I knew, spiraling down. Counting the parachutes . . . three, four, five. Five? Where were the others?

"Get out!" I'd shout. "Get out! Get out!"

As you can see, just talking about it, I am a little emotional. I choke up.

For years I didn't talk about the war with anybody—with one exception, my brother-in-law Leland. He was a navigational officer on the destroyer Cushing when she went down in the Pacific. He had shrapnel all up and down his right side. Lost his right eye. A fine man. We would get together during family vacations. Go down to the beach house, have a few snorts, and just sit there with our brandy bottle chit-chatting about our experiences. Our wives knew this was our time and they allowed us that.

I kept busy during those years. I had a great job as a sales representative. I was married to Jeane and we had a house and yard and children to look after. That's how I kept everything under control. I stayed busy. I had Leland to talk to. And I drank. I drank brandy, vodka martinis, whatever was available. Wine. If there was a table of people and they had a bottle of red and a bottle of white, I would count how many were drinking white and how many red. If more were drinking the white, I drank the red. If there was going to be more white, I'd drink that. It didn't make any difference to me, because by then I was an alcoholic.

When our first grandson was born, my daughter-in-law handed him to me in the hospital and said, "Here, Grandpa. Here's your first grandson." I had been drinking that day. My hands were shaking. I had grown up with sisters having babies; it was nothing for me to hold a baby or change a diaper, but when my daughter-in-law handed me my grandson, I was scared I'd drop him. That's when I said to myself, you've got to quit drinking. It was tough, but I managed to quit over the next few months. I haven't had a drink in decades.

A few years later, Leland died of cancer, and I had nobody to talk to. My sounding board was gone, my drinking crutch was gone, and everything that had happened to me during the war was backing up on me. I went into a depression. I was down, down, down. I could see no sense in living.

I found out about this prisoner of war program over at the VA hospital in Martinez, a support group for ex-POWs from the Pacific and European theaters. All World War II. I went, and at first I couldn't mention anybody—Art, Lou, Lowry, DiRocco—or talk about anything—the rifle butts in my back, Big Stoop, the Hitler Youth—without breaking down.

They sat there and listened. Nobody interrupted me. Nobody said I was taking too much time. "Hey, fella. Your fifteen minutes of fame are up." They didn't do that. Finally I could release it all. I could say, "I'm sharing this load with you. You're going to carry part of it." And this is what they did. When it was time to go home, everybody gave everybody a hug and said, "See you in two weeks."

Up until that point in time, 1988, I hadn't had anything to do with Art or Lou or anyone from my crew since the war. I had lost touch with everybody. I didn't want anything to do with the past, because every time I thought about somebody I would break down, and I thought, grown men don't cry. But I've learned since then that, hey, it's better if you do cry. Not talking about it, not breaking down is the worst thing in the world.

In 1989, I came across the name Lou Palermo in an ex-POW magazine. The magazine gave an address down in Orange county, so I wrote a letter asking, is this Lou Palermo? A letter came back, yes, it was Lou. I called him up. He was an electrical contractor in

Southern California, and he had an address for Art. I contacted Art and a few months later he telephoned to say he was in Walnut Creek. We arranged to meet the next day.

I thought this might be a story for the newspaper, so I called up the *Contra Costa Times* and told them Art and I had been in prison camp together and we hadn't seen each other in forty-four years. They sent a photographer and writer to cover the reunion.

Art and I agreed that we would never have been able to talk about things twenty or thirty years ago. It would have hurt much too much. Art was now an automotive writer going by the name of Dean Batchelor. After the war he actually built some of the hot rods we had dreamed up at Stalagluft IV. He had raced them on the flats at Salt Lake, and he was one of the first to clock two hundred miles an hour.

The day the story appeared in the *Times* I got another telephone call. It was from a man who lived a few miles from me, in Clayton. His name was Otto Groschwitz.

"I just read your article," he said. "It said you were shot down at Nuremberg."

"That's right."

"Well. I was a boy of fourteen in Nuremberg on the day your plane was shot down."

"Oh?"

"And as boys will do, my friends and I went out to the crash site and picked up pieces of the airplane as souvenirs."

"You did?"

"Yes. And I still have mine."

I was stunned. Here I was, the only member of my crew that lived on this side of the Mississippi, and this man who had a piece of my airplane was living just a few miles away. There is a force, I think, a bigger force than any of us can imagine, putting this all together.

Otto and his wife invited Jeane and me to their house. When we got there, he pulled out a map of Germany. "Well," he said. "It's been a long time, but I think the airplane came down here."

He touched the map. His finger was on the exact spot where the archives in Washington showed that my B-17 came down, about forty or fifty kilometers south of Nuremberg. Otto told us that the day after the crash he and his friends rode their bicycles out to the crash site. He found a scrap of aluminum from the plane and took it to a machinist friend, who cut it into a set of brass knuckles.

"Can I buy it from you?" I said.

"There is no amount of money that you could give me for this piece of your airplane," he said. "It doesn't belong to me. It is yours."

I grabbed him and hugged him. There were tears. I took the piece of metal home and framed it. I keep it right here in my office.

After that first visit, Jeane and I had many visits back and forth with Otto and his wife, and the four of us became good friends. Little by little my mind opened up about Germany and the Germans. I give God credit for that. Whether I knew it or not, from the day I jumped out of the B-17, all through my months as a POW and my years as an alcoholic, God was there the whole time.

For years I had said, "You'll never, ever get me back to Germany." I had so much hatred in me, I couldn't forgive. Then a friend of ours, a minister, sent us a brochure for a tour he was going to lead following Martin Luther's path though Germany. Jeane knew I wouldn't set foot in that country ever again, so when Stephen's brochure arrived in the mail, she thought, "Well, that's out," and she put it aside. She didn't even show it to me.

I found the brochure lying on Jeane's desk. I saw that Stephen's itinerary went right through the area I had marched with

Lou and Art in 1945. I told Jeane that if I was ever going to get over my bitterness and hatred of the Germans, this would be the time. Stephen knew my situation, and he would be there to help.

Jeane and I flew into Germany in 1990 with Stephen and a group of people from churches all around the U.S. In Frankfurt, we boarded a bus to Erfurt in East Germany. In the airport, in restaurants, on the street, wherever I'd hear German spoken, I'd startle and look around. I was jumpy.

One day when our bus was heading east, I saw a big sign over the highway. "Bitterfeld. Halle." I walked to the front of the bus and asked the driver, "Next time one of those big signs comes up, would you stop so I can get a picture?" He stopped. I got out of the bus and took the picture.

When I was back on the bus, Stephen came to where Jeane and I were sitting. "Everybody on the bus is curious about why you wanted that particular picture. Would you be up to telling them?"

I said I would, even though I had no idea how this was going to affect me. I went to the front of the bus, took the microphone, and sat down on a step facing the front window. I looked out at the countryside that I had walked, step by step, with hundreds of other men, and I started talking. I talked about being hungry and wet and sleeping out in the open fields. Remembrances of being kicked and hit with rifle butts came back to me. The old wounds opened up. I broke down. I cried. But I got through the whole story.

The bus was silent. I don't know how long I talked, but everyone listened. When I was through, I was exhausted. I went back to my seat, put my head against the window and fell asleep.

Our group spent that night in Leipzig, just a few miles from where I had been liberated. For the first time in forty-five years,

I slept the whole night through without waking up or having a nightmare. The next morning I couldn't remember a thing from the time I put my head down on the pillow until I woke up in the morning. After that, I saw Germany in color. In my mind, Germany wasn't black and white any more. I saw blue sky, green grass, red roofs. It was magical.

The Army Air Force officer at Santa Monica had been wrong. People can understand. You can share your story. There are plenty of nice people willing to take on part of your load. You don't have to carry it alone. So once again, the right thing happened to me at the right time. The good Lord picked that time for me to go back to Germany. He picked people for me to travel with, and he picked Stephen to lead the group.

Three years later, Jeane and I decided to visit Germany again. This time we wanted to travel to Nuremberg to look for the crash site of my old B-17 and see first-hand what had become of it. Thanks to Otto, I had an actual piece of my airplane and I knew roughly where it had ended up after Lowry, DiRocco, and the rest of us bailed out. The National Archives in Washington, D.C., keeps records of this kind of thing; the people there told me that the plane apparently stayed in automatic pilot and continued south in a long, slow downward glide. It finally settled to the ground about nine kilometers northeast of a place called Weissenburg and one kilometer northwest of another place called Laubenthal.

Jeane and I contacted the travel bureau in Weissenburg and explained that we would be in Germany, staying in a hotel in Nuremberg. We wanted to look at the place where the plane crashed, and if somebody in the area remembered the incident, we would like to talk to them. When we arrived at our hotel, a letter from the travel bureau was waiting for us with the telephone number of Fritz and Berta Huttinger. I called the number. Fritz spoke a little English, and I could make it understood that we would be in Weissenburg the next day.

We met at the travel agency, had lunch, and piled into Fritz's car, along with Fritz's teenaged niece, who had studied English and could help translate. We drove to a *Gasthof*, a good-sized roadhouse and hotel just outside Laubenthal. Fritz's father used to own the *Gasthof*, Fritz said, and his father had been there when the airplane came in, low and steady, over a hill to the north. It had settled into the woods on the family property, just behind the *Gasthof*. There was no explosion or fire.

Apparently my friend back in Clayton, Otto Groschwitz, and his buddies weren't the only local boys to rush to the scene. According to Fritz, another boy climbed into the plane. Inside, he found a forty-five caliber handgun, mine or DiRocco's probably, and shot off two of his fingers.

Fritz drove his car about a quarter mile off the main road into a little forest. We parked, got out of the car and stood there looking at the trees. By 1993, nothing was left of the airplane itself. It had been scrapped during the war and made into German fighter planes, Folkwolf 190s and Messerschmidt 109s. But a seventy-five-foot Flying Fortress doesn't crash to the ground without leaving a mark on the landscape, and right away I could see where our B-17 had hit. To the back and around the outside of the woods, the trees were tall and still intact. In the middle of the woods directly in front of us were the remnants of broken tree trunks. A huddle of smaller, newer trees was growing up.

I closed my eyes. I could visualize the B-17 gliding into that spot, crushing the trees as it settled in. I said to the girl, "Tell your uncle that the reason we had to abandon the airplane was that we were hit with anti-aircraft fire over Nuremberg. We lost three engines and we had to bail out." I watched while she translated.

Fritz looked kind of surprised. Then he looked at me. In careful English he said, "On the day you were shot down, I was on an anti-aircraft gun in Nuremberg. I was sixteen years old."

We just looked at each other. It was such a feeling. Here I was, standing there admitting to Fritz that I had bombed Nuremberg. And Fritz was standing there admitting to me that he was on the ground, shooting up at me and my buddies. We threw our arms around each other and cried like babies.

That day was just one more part of my healing. And Fritz's too, I think, because I am pretty sure that he needed it as much as I did. In 1944, we were trying to kill each other. And now all these years later, we are friends. When we see each other, we hug and kiss each other on the cheek. Every year we send Christmas cards.

I feel like I have finally completed my eighteenth mission. I'm easy with my thoughts and with my God. As far as holding a grudge, there is no such thing anymore. On the day I was shot down, I stood there with my parachute and nothing but blue sky in front of me, and all I could think of was, I'm in God's hands now. And I was.

As many times as I've damned God, he has been there. Sure, I hollered at him and yelled at him, and he knew I damned well meant it. But the good Lord was there for me all that time. Giving me strength on the march to go one more mile. Giving me saviors like Lou and Art. And a wife like Jeane. And friends like the POW support group and Stephen and the church people on the Germany tour. Giving me Lowry and DiRocco and the other men in my B-17 crew that I've managed to locate. Giving me Otto and Fritz.

9

A Good God? Maybe, Maybe Not

Robert Tharratt chooses to put his trust in God. But some skeptics would point to Robert's suffering as a sign of God's non-existence. They would ask how God, who is supposed to be both loving and all-powerful, can permit so much evil—war, murder, injustice and slavery, and earthquakes, tornados, disease and death. Philosophers call this age-old question "the problem of evil," and it goes like this: if there is suffering in the world, then God is either not good, not all-powerful—or non-existent.

But I would say: what kind of God are we talking about here?

While at the *Contra Costa Times*, I interviewed a young man named Rezwan Pavri, who would later go on to become an attorney and partner at a large national law firm. Rezwan is an adherent of Zoroastrianism, an ancient Middle Eastern tradition that teaches that God is not all-powerful. "We believe God to be all-loving, but not all-powerful," Rezwan told me. A second, evil force in the universe is responsible for human suffering, he said, a force that in the end will give way to God and God's army for the good—humanity.

Rezwan's story sheds interesting light on the problem of evil. So does George Strong's. George is a Christian Scientist and the administrator of a Christian Science nursing facility in suburban Castro Valley. Christian Science, he explained, teaches that it is not God, but *suffering*—disease and death—that is not real.

"Man was made in the likeness of God," he said. "In that likeness, it seems plain that sickness and disease and even death have no place." Consequently, like many Christian Scientists, George seeks help for his injuries and illnesses through prayer, not medical care. And, too, when George celebrates a birthday, it is in celebration of a person, not the anniversary of the beginning of that person's life. An anniversary marks time and, for George, time is no more real than matter.

In other words, Christian Scientists like George solve the problem of evil by asserting that human suffering is an illusion. Zoroastrians like Rezwan assert that God is not all-powerful. And atheists like Christopher Hitchens, Richard Dawkins, and Anthony Mack argue that there is simply no God.

Which leaves the problem of evil's one other premise—God's so-called just and compassionate nature. Breathes there a human being who dares to call God's goodness into question?

Yes, there is.

I first met Elizabeth Felts when she was senior minister at Danville Congregational Church, an affluent congregation in an upscale suburb. Her church's newsletter arrived in my in-box at the *Contra Costa Times* on a regular basis. One month the newsletter announced that Elizabeth was taking time off work. Her pregnancy had ended in a stillbirth. She had lost a child, a son.

I pored over the announcement. I couldn't help wondering, how does a pastor, a person upon whom hundreds of people depend for spiritual leadership, hold on to her trust in God through the pain of such a loss? In my case, just the possibility of losing Christina had pretty much finished off what was left of my youthful belief in a loving, compassionate God.

I waited a few months then called and asked Elizabeth for an interview. Without hesitation, she invited me to her office at Danville Congregational Church so that I could put my question to her in person. Elizabeth was a trim, petite woman—a daily runner I learned later. Her diminutive figure was dwarfed by her office's expansive, oversized executive desk, and I couldn't help imagining that the furniture in this office had been installed with a grander, probably male, pastor in mind. But Elizabeth was not easily daunted. She took her place behind the desk, offered me a chair across the room, and told her story.

During that first interview, Elizabeth was composed, ministerial. But when we met again several years later and Elizabeth resumed her story, I learned to my surprise that her mood had shifted: her ideas about God's goodness were as tentative and wary as my own.

Elizabeth's story begins as mine did, when an unborn baby suddenly goes quiet.

Elizabeth Chandler Felts—Her Story

My baby was dead. This was my second pregnancy. It had been perfectly normal until about half way through, when I became aware that I hadn't felt the baby move in two or three days. I went in for an ultrasound. The technician ran the transducer across my stomach, her eyes fixed on the monitor screen, looking for the baby's heartbeat. The transducer slid across my stomach, back and forth, back and forth. Ten minutes went by. No heartbeat. Nothing.

The next day, the doctors induced labor. I had twenty hours of awful contractions, followed by hemorrhaging. It was a son. He was eleven inches long, just under a pound, and perfectly formed. He had been dead three or four days, so his skin was purple and peeling. Otherwise, he looked like a normal baby. Fingers, toes, ears, chin.

I was the pastor at Danville Congregational Church at the time. My husband was out of town, but three deacons from my church came to my bedside. They were there in minutes. They took turns holding the baby and speaking words of love to him. Technically, I knew, baptism was a sacrament for the living, not for the dead, but I wanted to bring this baby fully into the circle of Christians who would have loved him—who *had* loved him. So, sitting in the hospital bed and using ordinary tap water from the sink in my room, I baptized my son.

At first, God and I were just fine. It seemed to me that my son's death was just one of the tragedies that occur in life. I didn't ask why. I didn't think to let it embitter me or damage my relationship with God. The people in our congregation would not let me lose faith with God. They held me and cried with me. They fed my husband, my two-year-old daughter, and me for weeks. They visited us and prayed with us. Hundreds of cards came in the mail. They said, "You take the time you need and don't come back to work until you are ready."

The people of our church incarnated Christ for me in every imaginable way. It wasn't possible to lose faith with a God who was that constant. A personal relationship with Jesus is important in some strata, but not to me. That hymn, "What a Friend We Have in Jesus," doesn't speak to me. Being Christ for someone and accepting someone being Christ for me, that's about as close as I get.

After three weeks, I returned to work. I felt fine. I jumped right back into things. I thought, I'll replace this child soon; it won't be long before I have another baby to hold, and that will cure my grieving. I pushed any troubling thoughts aside, and trusted in God's providential care. Every night I prayed a prayer of childish innocence with my daughter, my surviving child. "Now I lay me down to sleep. I pray thee God, thy child to keep."

I grew up in Marion, a small mining town in southern Illinois, right on the buckle of the Bible Belt. My friends all went to the First, Second, Third, Fourth, Fifth, Sixth, or Seventh Baptist Church. My family attended one of the few mainline churches in town. But religion wasn't talked about at our house. The only time we had a family prayer was at Sunday dinner. It was a silent prayer. My father would drop his hands to his lap, bow his head, and ten seconds later raise his head. That was it. We didn't even say amen. The prayer was over. My mother would pick up her fork and we could eat.

But I was different. I was fascinated with churchly things—hymns, organ music, scripture, the sacraments. When I was fourteen I started going to a fundamentalist Pentecostal church and underwent a conversion. That's what I called it. The day after my conversion—the laying on of hands and the speaking in tongues—I sat down at the breakfast table with my father and mother.

"How did the evening go?" they asked.

"I found Jesus."

Aside from my father sputtering in his coffee, my parents didn't say a thing. To their great credit, they didn't try to discourage me. They drove me to prayer meeting every Sunday and Wednesday and to revival all summer long. I think they understood that it was a hunger I had.

My mother was diagnosed with cancer when I was eleven, and she deteriorated steadily until her agonizing death five years later. I continued on in the Pentecostal church after that. But once I got to college, I did a flip-flop and started going to Catholic and Anglican churches. I was one of the few women in my sorority of party girls at Northwestern who got up on Sunday morning to go to church. I wanted to experience this thing called the Mass, so I pretended to be Catholic. I watched people to see how it was done, then I followed them to the altar for communion. I was checking it all out, like "Goldilocks and the Three Bears."

Eventually, I transferred my affections to the United Church of Christ, which was proactive in social justice and in ordaining women. I studied at Harvard Divinity School, a deconstructionist seminary that took me apart like a clock, and I loved it. They challenged every dearly held belief I'd ever had.

Did Jesus make the blind man see? Did he really turn water into wine? I found out that these were the wrong questions. The real question was: What was it about Jesus that made people believe he could turn water into wine? Who was this man who made people feel they were in the presence of God? By reframing my beliefs, I survived divinity school with my faith intact, and in 1987 I was ordained.

For the six years following the stillbirth of our son, my husband and I tried to have another baby. I got pregnant two more times. Each time, I saw the baby's heartbeat on the ultrasound at the doctor's office. Each time, I miscarried in the third month. My husband and I kept trying until I was forty-five years old. Fertility drugs. In vitro fertilization. Acupuncture. Asian herbs. Homeopathy. We tried everything.

Again and again our efforts were rewarded with a great, echoing "No!" from God. I felt so . . . flayed. God had taken away my son, and now God was taking away my fertility, my means of replacing him. There was definitely something twisted in that. My image of God darkened. Why would a good, omnipotent God allow bad things to happen? Try as I might, I can't hold all the pieces of that equation together. Something has to give. The author Rabbi Harold Kushner says that "omnipotent" is the piece that has to drop out. God's hands, ultimately, are tied. But I say, of what use is such a God? How much more frightening is it if God is not really in control?

I have seen in my own life how terrible God's power actually is. Against all my liberal conditioning, I have come to believe in a God who chooses not to prevent evil, who perhaps even visits evil upon creation and its creatures. It's a monstrous idea, but a biblical one. The Hebrew scriptures give many snapshots of a vengeful, punishing God who wipes out entire populations: Noah and the Flood, Sodom and Gomorrah. And a violent God shows up in Christian scriptures as well: what kind of father deliberately sacrifices his son on a cross?

Even more monstrous than this vision of God is the fact that I go right on being faithful to such a deity. Attending church. Teaching Sunday school children. Preaching the gospel. Why? Maybe I'd rather haggle it out with an imperfect God than live a life without faith. Maybe it's easier to put up with a lot of unanswered questions and a lot of irony than to set my tradition aside.

Under God's watch, my heart has been hurt, and I don't like it. But I won't walk away from God. I won't walk away from the table. As a good Congregationalist, I have learned to endure a lot of tension and a lot of uncertainty in a relationship. I'm not afraid of edginess. I have suspended the need to have all my questions answered. There is an inscrutable, unsettling complexity to God, which the contemporary Christian church is ill-prepared to interpret to its flock. So much of Christianity today is one simple-minded variation or another on "God is love." But one thing's sure: God is not simple.

Meanwhile, I take nothing for granted. I have lost so much— mother, children, fertility, innocence, simplicity. I no longer walk down life's dark streets without glancing right and left to see what's coming at me. Every time I embrace my daughter, and I do mean every time, I breathe in the scent of her hair and I think to myself, this could be the last time I embrace her. Every time my husband gets ready to take a plane half way around the world to do business, I look him in the eye and memorize his face.

10

Justice Isn't Part of the Grand Scheme

As I listened to the stories of people like Elizabeth Felts, Robert Tharratt, and Charles Townes, something started to become clear to me. Something obvious. And that was that God—and human suffering—is beyond human understanding. God is big. To my surprise, it was not a hefty Christian theologian or a learned Jewish rabbi who was finally able to put that—humbling—thought into words for me. It was a Witch.

Cerridwen Fallingstar lives in the tiny roadside town of San Geronimo, in Marin county north of San Francisco and not far from the Pacific Ocean. She practices Wicca and describes herself as a shamanic Witch and priestess. She is also the author of *The Heart of the Fire*, a novel set in sixteenth-century Scotland, and the *White as Bone, Red as Blood* novels, set in twelfth-century Japan.

I arrived in San Geronimo for a visit with Cerridwen on a rain-soaked winter day. The grass in her front yard was wet, and my shoes were damp and muddy by the time I reached the front door of her small house. When I knocked, a slender, fit woman in her forties with fine features and cascading, blond hair opened the door to welcome me in. I stepped across the threshold and found myself in Cerridwen's living room, standing on her carpet in my wet shoes. She asked me to take the shoes off, which I did. Spotting my damp, nylon-stockinged toes, Cerridwen disappeared into another room and returned with a blanket. After seating me at her dining room table, she gently wrapped the blanket around my legs and feet.

Like Elizabeth, Cerridwen had lost a pregnancy, a daughter, a few years earlier. Then, just days after the miscarriage, her husband, a hospital nurse, succumbed unexpectedly to a raging infection—hemolytic strep—and died within a week.

"I'm not all here," she told me. "It's like I have one foot in the other world, the spirit world, and can't find my way back."

Cerridwen's story begins with a love affair.

Cerridwen Fallingstar—Her Story

I remember my conception. My parents were making love outdoors in this beautiful garden. They were having the best time. My parents had a deep passion for each other, and I know that's why I picked them out. I got really lucky, I was brought up in a household with two people who were madly in love. My mother and father were living in southern California when I was born. They were agnostic, scientific people—my father worked with computers back in the days when a computer took up an entire room—and I was the little black sheep in this rational family. From the time I was young, I was a totally spiritual person. My mother tells me I'd go out and talk to the birds and the animals in the garden.

When I was three or four years old, there was a tarantula that lived under the house. She was furry looking, very pettable, and she would come up and sit next to me on the porch. I knew that I couldn't touch her, because if I reached out my hand, she would edge away. But we would have conversations.

When I first started talking, it was witches this and witches that. I could not stop talking about witches. My parents took me to see *Snow White* when I was about three. All through the movie, the witch is portrayed as evil. At the end, when the people are driving her off the cliff, I started screaming. "No, no, she's good. She's really good." My parents had to take me out of the theater.

My family didn't talk about religion much when I was a child. We went camping a lot, and my father had a rather Pagan attitude. He would say, "Why would anybody go to church when they could go sit with the trees?" Later, when kids were asking me what church my family went to, my dad said, "Tell them we're a bunch of Pagans. Tell them we worship the trees." I totally related to that. Being outdoors, that's where I feel the connection with whatever you want to call it—God or Goddess or "the force that through the green fuse drives the flower." That force, that power, that beautiful connection, mostly I get it from being in nature.

What is God like? What is Spirit? Danged if I know. My brain isn't big enough. I'm never going to get it, I have to accept that. But I can love it, I can appreciate it, I can honor it. I don't understand how it works, but a thread in a tapestry doesn't understand its position in the tapestry either. I can't understand it, but I feel it.

When I was twenty-two, I finally met some Witches and got to do my life path. Up until then, everything I had heard was that the Witches were all dead—they had been killed, wiped out in Europe—and it was over.

I was working as a newspaper reporter in Los Angeles, on a feminist newspaper called *Together*, and my editor came in and said, "There's this Witch, Z Budapest, on trial for fortune telling."

I said, "That's my story. I'll take that story."

That was Z Budapest's trial for fortune telling in 1975. So I worked with her and her coven for about six months. Later, I started my own coven. A coven is a small group of Witches, usually thirteen people or fewer. It's not a congregation with a minister. It's like an extended family, which makes it a very intimate setting for spiritual exploration. I was just lucky to run into Z Budapest. It wasn't like a conversion. It was, "Ah. Whew. I can come home now. Finally, I can do what I'm supposed to do."

It's traditional in Wicca to take a spiritual name. The Fallingstar—during my first summer solstice ritual, in 1975, I looked up and saw a falling star. The Cerridwen is for Cerridwen, the goddess of transformation and inspiration in Celtic mythology.

Z Budapest was convicted, she never denied reading the fortune. But from all that, the Covenant of the Goddess began. It's an umbrella organization for Witches all over the country, and I'm a legal minister in it. I teach magic and ritual and I do individual sessions using hypnosis and psychic readings.

Witches are what is left of the old European Goddess cultures, which honored the earth as the body of the living Goddess, the Mother Earth. Unfortunately, not much of the record of Pagan culture and ritual is left. We have a little from this source or that source, but a lot is reconstructed. There's a blessing to that. A religious tradition stays fresh if you keep reinventing it. A Wiccan elder I know said, "I practice exactly the way my ancestors did sixty thousand years ago. I make it up."

I lost my husband a few years ago. That same week I had a miscarriage, a baby girl. And my dad died in a car accident at age fifty. Parts of me have died. The woman who was married to her true love since she was seventeen years old has died. The woman who was to be mother to a living daughter has died. And now, here I am at mid-life, my son, my surviving child has gone off to college, and I'm losing my fertility. Things have been taken from me. I've had a lot of losses.

My husband was the healthiest man on earth, and then this bacterial infection killed him in a week. He went from being totally healthy to being dead in one week. Sometimes nature doesn't care how many vegetables you eat. Whatever is out there in the spiritual realm doesn't see things the way we see them. Justice does not seem to be part of the grand scheme. Even the food we eat is mostly things that have died, so that even if you are a vegetarian you are eating death. Whatever God is, it's something that doesn't operate the way we do.

There is a Rumi poem I like. Coleman Barks translated it. It's called, "The Dream That Must Be Interpreted."

> *This place is a dream.*
> *Only a sleeper considers it real . . .*
> *Then death comes like dawn,*
> *And you wake up laughing*
> *At what you thought was your grief.*

Of course we don't understand why we have to die, and why we suffer. We are people. Yet we want everything to make sense according to us. And that's where fanaticism comes from—from needing to be certain that God sees things the way we do. Humility is realizing that we don't see the world the way God does.

My husband was the love of my life, just as the earth is the love of my life, and Spirit is the love of my life. Some of my most intense spiritual experiences were making love to my husband and feeling that union with all things. Looking in his eyes was like looking into the eyes of the cosmos.

Those high moments, those satori moments, that's what gives our lives meaning. Who knows how the universe works? I don't. I do not have a clue. What's important is that you let yourself have the full experience of love with your partner and your children, and with Spirit. You may not understand the divine, but that doesn't mean you don't get to experience it.

My parents were nuts about each other. It was an agnostic household, but there was a lot of intimacy happening. And really, what is Spirit? If you get to have love, how can God be far behind?

PART FIVE: *Humanity's Problem—*
Choosing the Good

11

A Theology of Babies Born Without Brains

God is big. God is beyond human understanding. And if Cerridwen Fallingstar has it right, God lives outside the human categories of good and evil. But how about humans? Are we good? Do we have the wherewithal to be ethical? Can we choose to be good?

As Charles Townes points out, most of us human beings, including even the most rigorous of scientists, act as though we have free choice and can make moral decisions. But can we? As human beings, do we have choices? Or are we completely at the mercy of our genetic heritage? Are we predestined by our biology to act selfishly, cruelly even, in our own best interests? Or do we have something like a soul that lifts us above our animal instinct for self-preservation?

I'd like to think that Martin Luther King, Jr., got it right when he said, "the arc of the moral universe is long, but it bends toward justice." Geoff Machin and René Molho share my hope. Both men have seen the dark side of things—Geoff in the doomed children he sees in his practice as a pediatric pathologist; René in his own behavior, good and evil, during two and a half years of internment at Auschwitz-Birkenau during World War II.

Despite their clear vision of the cruelty of the universe, both

men take the side of hope, hope that human beings are capable—
at least some of the time—of living up to their ideals of generosity and compassion. From them I learned to hope, to trust, that
my choices do indeed matter. That it matters what I do. That although I cannot know for sure what God is—if God is at all—and
although as time goes by I will inevitably suffer misfortune, loss,
and sooner or later death, I am entitled to do and act and be the
way I want the universe to be. That is my birthright.

Geoff Machin gave me fair warning. When I first telephoned
him to ask for an interview, he informed me that he was a
tough-minded physician and scientist who embraced a stripped-
down version of Christianity. "I don't practice my religion at the
brain stem or the emotional level," he said. "I see my religion as a
synthesis of the hard sciences."

Unlike Cerridwen Fallingstar and so many others I've met
along the way, Geoff does not see nature as a nurturing, sustaining expression of God. For Geoff, the natural world is a bloodbath.
Every creature on earth, including humans, "is locked in a deadly struggle with every other individual—within the species and
across the species."

Even our DNA is unreliable, he told me when we sat down to
talk. The process of copying DNA from one cell to another is a
sloppy one. That sloppiness permits mutations to slip through,
and it is the basis for the evolution of the species. But it's also
the basis of genetic disease, including cancer. "You can't have one
without the other."

At the time of our first interview, Geoff was working at the Kaiser Permanente Medical Center in Oakland, and living with his
wife Ann in a small, wood-frame cottage in the city's hilly Mont-
clair district. The cottage's sunroom looked out into the remnants
of a plum orchard. Just beyond the orchard was St. John's Epis-

copal Church, my own home church, where Ann was the office administrator and Geoff sang in the choir. An Oxford-educated Englishman, Geoff was dressed casually in slacks and a red crew neck sweater frayed around the collar. His brown beard and mustache covered most of his mouth. His blue eyes gleamed from behind gold-rimmed glasses, which were oversized, squarish, and a couple of years out of style.

Geoff's story begins in the spiraled strands of DNA that are the blueprints for the next generation of human life. More often than not, Geoff told me, an individual blueprint is flawed and a young life is doomed.

Geoff Machin—His Story

Part of my job is to go down into the depths of hell with parents. The wife is pregnant. The couple has bought a larger house. They've got the crib and the diapers. They've had all the tests. And now their obstetrician and I have to tell them that their unborn baby has a big hole in its brain.

As a fetal and genetic pathologist, I deliver a lot of bad news every week. Some newborn infants I see have nothing worse than a clubfoot, which can be put straight with splints. Others have simple heart disease, which can respond to surgery. But some have truly severe problems. No brain. No kidneys. Spina bifida. Terrible malformations of the heart or the lungs. Some will live in a persistent vegetative state in institutions, fed by a tube in the stomach, surviving bout after bout of pneumonia, and costing society maybe a million dollars a year.

Affluent North Americans often lose sight of how precarious human existence truly is. We have this idea that every child is going to ride a Razor scooter. He's going to be a millionaire; she's going to go to college. It's because of this stupid, optimistic society we live in. Our secular culture tells us, just be cheerful and

it'll work out. If we take care of ourselves, if there's enough quality control, our children will be born perfect like so many washing machines coming off the assembly line. But the concept that
every human being will be a Cadillac is an idolatry, isn't it? It's the
false god of pseudo-perfection. In reality so many children suffer,
babes and sucklings.

The human beings who are alive today are the tip of the ice-
berg. They got born and most of them are in pretty good shape,
but underneath them are millions and millions of conceptuses
that did not make it. Perhaps 80 percent of the human beings
conceived have major genetic problems and never see the light of
day. The redemptive feature in all this is that when parents learn
they have conceived a malformed child, they often grow deeper
because of it, they realize their frailty. They are relieved of the
burden of thinking that everything they touch must be perfect.

That's the kind of stuff I do all week. Often I can be of help,
but mostly it's a lot of bad news. But it's reality. Reality is the rock
upon which I stand. I know what the world is like; we are physically imperfect, all of us. We were not created by God and put
here one at a time as perfect human beings, as copies of God. We
are the products of millennia of Darwinian competition, which
only the fittest survive. This frailty, this Darwinian imperfection
of ours, has got to be incorporated somehow into our theology.

We need a theology of children born with no brains: Who is
this God who allows genes to be imperfect? Why doesn't he just
produce a nice zebra and a nice baby every time? For that matter,
why does God permit poverty, hunger, disease, and war? To me,
this is a profound mystery.

I was born at home in Sutton on the south side of London in
1940, a dreadful time, six or nine months into the Second World
War. I spent the first weeks of my life in an air raid shelter in a

wicker laundry basket in the dark while all hell raged overhead. My earliest memories are of war. On the mornings after an air raid, my schoolmates and I would walk to school looking for spent anti-aircraft fire, which we called shrapnel, bits of steel that had melted in the sky and dropped to the ground. We'd see who could get to school with the most shrapnel, then we'd trade them the way American kids trade baseball cards. "I'll give you this one for those two." On some days a house would be missing along the way. It had been there yesterday, now it was gone and everyone was dead.

My parents were nominal Church of England Christians; for them going to church once a month was enough. But I had religious education at school once a week and I learned a lot of scripture, which is still part of me: "The wolf shall dwell with the lamb, and the leopard shall lie down with the kid. They shall not hurt nor destroy in all my holy mountain."

When I was growing up, there was this dreadful thing, the Eleven Plus exam, that all children took after their eleventh birthdays. Pages and pages of horrendous multiple choice stuff that you had to do at top speed. Unless your parents were very rich, the Eleven Plus determined the rest of your life. If you came from an average, lower middle class family like myself—my family owned an educational supply business that didn't turn over a big profit—and you passed the Eleven Plus, you could go to a grammar school, which would prepare you for something like the trades or banking or teaching. You might even qualify for a university education. If you did not pass the Eleven Plus, you went to a thing called secondary school and you would be a tiller of the soil and a drawer of water till the end of your days. Even as a boy I could see the dreadful effect it had on children who failed it by only a point or two. It troubles me still, so many damaged and wasted lives.

My parents were ambitious for me, and like a lot of other middle class parents, they had me coached to take that exam. They were absolutely deliriously happy when I got into a very superior grammar school. For them the purpose of my education from now on was to get me kitted up to go to university. To stay on the top of the competitive heap, I had to specialize and grow quickly in one area of knowledge—in my case the sciences. There wasn't time to hang around with friends, there was scarcely time to talk to my parents. Yet it was a wonderful education. By the time I was fourteen, I was doing high-powered biology, chemistry, and physics.

I can still remember the day my chemistry teacher explained the Periodic Table of Elements. "Hydrogen has one proton in the atom," he said. "Helium has two, lithium three, beryllium four, and so on." I thought, wonderful, what a revelation. Hydrogen, helium, lithium, beryllium, boron, carbon, nitrogen, oxygen. It had an underlying pattern that to me was rational and beautiful.

In 1953, when I was thirteen, Watson and Crick announced the double helix, the structure of the DNA genetic code. The newspapers were full of the story, and it was an epiphany for me. It put two questions into sharp relief: Is there a God and what is God like? And second, why are humans the way we are? Are we good, bad, or what? I thought Darwinism and the double helix might give us some answers. That's when I knew I wanted to do human genetics as my career.

When I went to Oxford in 1959, it was still part of a magical, aristocratic world. People went there, generation after generation, because they could afford it, because they came from the right family, and because they had been educated at one of the exclusive schools. And there I was, a lower-middle-class kid from the mean streets of suburban London. I had never seen the second son of an earl in my life, and I couldn't talk about my family's house in the country because we didn't have one.

Very few children of the middle classes broke into Oxford in those days. I can't help thinking, if my parents and my school hadn't groomed me for university, somebody else from the mean streets of somewhere else in Britain might have gone to Oxford in my place. Even now I carry a pack of guilt on my back about that, and I often wonder, what has happened to that other person? I came out of Oxford, not a communist, but a bright red socialist, and I've remained so ever since. I am totally opposed to elites. We are all children of God. The idea is to do good in the world; it's not to belong to groups or live in big executive houses.

After Oxford, I spent three years in medical school and ten years in residency working at a medical specialty that did not yet exist—human genetic pathology. I studied malformations, chromosomal abnormalities, all the things that can go wrong in pregnancy. Ann and I married and we had two boys. Twelve years later, to our parents' dismay, we left for Calgary, Canada, where we thrived. A few years ago, Kaiser Permanente head-hunted me to come down here to the States as the regional fetal genetic pathologist for Kaiser.

Which means that, a half-century after Watson and Crick discovered the double helix, I am still working at synthesizing religion with science and Darwinism. To do that, I have had to give up some aspects of the old religion that do not stand up to scientific scrutiny. One is that human life began in harmony in the Garden of Eden and that it is the fault of humans that the world and human beings are no longer good. Another is that God controls earthly events, including evolution and the fate of individuals. Those metaphysical constructs don't work for me anymore.

The fact is, we humans are the products of millions of years of evolution. We were not created "good" or "innocent." Like every other plant and animal on earth, we are deeply competitive, and we always have been. Warfare rages throughout all of animal and plant life. Human beings, the whole of biology, groans in competition, and yet—despite knowing what we know now about quantum mechanics, the big bang, human genetics, and natural selection—many Christians still revere the book of Genesis and the Garden of Eden as if it is all we've got to go on and must be literally believed.

Many of us cling to a pre-Darwinian, eighteenth- and nineteenth-century concept of the natural world that says, "Isn't nature beautiful? Look out there, look at the sun on those trees, look at the green against the blue sky, and look at the red of that plum tree. Beautiful! And, look, there's a squirrel."

I call this concept the romantic model. What the romantic model doesn't tell you is that the plum tree grew from a pit that was one of thousands shed by another tree. Of those thousands of plum pits, only the one survived. The romantic model doesn't tell you that the squirrel is flea-ridden and has intestinal parasites. It's got chronic diarrhea from the parasites, and it's scratching itself all the time because of the fleas. It's not living a happy life. The romantic model doesn't explain why birds abandon a nest after two or three years. Why do they? Because the nest is crawling with parasites. Their newborns would never survive that high level of ticks and fleas and mites, so they go elsewhere and build a new one.

Every tree, every animal, every bacterium, and every virus on earth is locked in a deadly struggle with every other individual—within the species and across the species. There is a constant waxing and waning of competition in a world with limited nutrients, limited space, limited air, light, and water. Anything that doesn't compete goes to the wall and dies. There is slaughter everywhere.

When a new male becomes dominant in a troop of chimpanzees, his first job is to kill off the youngest male offspring because they carry the genes of the previous dominant male, not his.

And it's clear to me that genocide is a part of human nature as well. The Holocaust is just one instance of it. We've seen genocide in Rwanda. We've seen it in Israel, and in Sierra Leone and Nigeria. Why? It has to do with the survival of one clan over another. There is room for only so many people in a given ecological niche; it's us or them.

Nature is cruel and competitive. "Red in tooth and claw"—isn't that what Alfred Lord Tennyson said of Darwinism? That plum tree exists because a thousand others do not. Billions of salmon hatchlings are born each year, of which 1 percent might reach the sea, the rest are eaten or drown. Far, far more bacteria and insects and animals and plants are born than can ever survive. This extreme overproduction of fertilized seeds and eggs occurs in every species throughout nature, including humans.

I remember driving to an event with some friends. Lo and behold, somebody pulled out of a parking spot just as we were coming along. "Oh, I must have deserved that," said the driver, really quite believing it. "I must have said my prayers this week." And do you remember that fire down in Los Angeles? Whole neighborhoods of houses were destroyed. One house was left standing, and the owner was interviewed on television. "There must be a God," she said, pointing to her house.

I say that's pietistic rubbish. What about the people whose houses burned to the ground? God doesn't work that way, it seems to me. He doesn't. I've seen too much suffering and sorrow and pain in my work. I don't know what God is, but I do know what God isn't. The world isn't fair. God has not counted every hair on your head, he doesn't know about every swallow that falls from the sky, he doesn't keep people's houses from burning down, and he certainly doesn't find parking places for believers.

I would say that if God created the world, he does not control it to the extent we like to think. God must be operating on a macro scale, he's not micromanaging, as I see the evidence. If he did create the universe, he created what seems to be a mathematical, atomic-type world. Intrinsic in the whole system is much imperfection, much waste. Plum pits. Salmon hatchlings that don't make it to the open ocean. Babies who die in utero. That poor other fellow in England who didn't go to Oxford and didn't get the chance to do what I'm doing.

So, here we are, at the beginning of a new millennium, living out our biological history, which we can't just dump—but maybe it's our job to dump it. Maybe God created this system so that human beings would transcend it. If we are to transcend our nature, our theology must first take on board what it's like to be an animal, to be human. And that is, to accept that we are fundamentally selfish. We strive to survive. We strive to reproduce, which is why we wear sharp suits and put on lipstick and do all the sexual attraction things. We can fully explain, in Darwinian terms, why we behave like the turds we do. It's our nature.

A psychology researcher sat in a parking lot one day observing people as they came back to their cars. The idea was to measure how much time went by between unlocking the door and actually driving out of the parking spot. Did the driver take more or less time to back out if somebody was waiting for the spot?

The answer is yes, it does matter. If someone is waiting for your parking spot, you dawdle! If no one is waiting, you go faster. That's pure Darwinism. Your parking spot is an ecological niche: You're a sea anemone in a nice crevice in the rock. Another creature comes along. Do you let it in? Of course not.

Jesus said things like, "If somebody wants your coat, let him have your shirt also." And, "Love your enemies. Do good to those who hate you." Jesus understood our biological nature very well. He understood that we are naturally selfish. That is the reason he was incarnated, so that he could have full human characteristics, which he then transcended.

Our job if we are to be Christ-like is to follow his commandment to love one another and transcend our brutish nature—and recognize the true magnitude of the task. Could that be God's wish for the world? That human beings overcome their Darwinian origins, as Christ suggested? If we were to actually do that, might we then be headed toward an upland where, "They shall no more hurt nor destroy in all my holy mountain"? Is that what the world could be?

Human beings are the only living things that know they exist and ask why. We'd probably have more fun if we didn't ask so many questions, just go to the beach and have a beer. Well, some of us do bother about these things, we live with the questions. That is the God in us, I think. That is the extent to which we are made in God's image. The very fact that so many people push toward a meaningful basis for their lives is, to me, evidence of God's existence.

All around me I see people feeding the homeless or volunteering to travel half way around the world to vaccinate children for polio in places like Angola, Pakistan, or Afghanistan. I think of the Jubilee movement, which campaigned to have international debt forgiven in Third World countries so that the money could be spent on education and health. Because of that, creditors wrote off billions of dollars of debt. And I think of Dr. Matthew Lukwiya, who returned to his hospital in Gula, Uganda, to help control an outbreak of the Ebola virus. He could have stayed away, but he didn't. He caught the virus and died.

This is all tremendously anti-biological. This is highly vicarious behavior. We're talking about systemic neighborliness here. It's not tit for tat, and it defies common sense. The Darwinian approach would be, "Let them die." And yet there is something in some people that makes them say, "We're going to go over there and help those people."

Could this behavior be a footprint of God? Could the way we are and the way we think come from God? The answer has to be yes. I can't explain these things in any other way. Yes, there are babies born without brains. Yes, nature is red in tooth and claw. And yet I see God's love and grace every day in the generosity of the people around me. It's that grace that opens our eyes to the needs of others and allows us to overcome our Darwinian origins. That's how I reconcile science and religion: I accept the Darwinian model of creation, and yet I am a believing Christian working in a frail and fragile humanity.

12

"The One Bad Thing I Did"

For many years, René Molho took pride in declaring himself an atheist. "What kind of God would allow the Holocaust?" he would say. "How could I believe in such a God? I'm not Job." By the time I met René, however, which was a few years before he died, he had mellowed a bit on the God question. "Maybe there is a need in the human being to believe in something," he conceded. "If you are born nothing and you die nothing, it's an empty life." Either way, God remained something of an abstraction for René. He was at heart a humanist and a moralist. People mattered to him: His family, the people of his synagogue, humanity in general—and children.

When on a September afternoon, I arrived at the door of his spotless condominium in suburban Alameda, the cul-de-sac was noisy with children playing ball in the street. René smiled as he took in the commotion. "I wouldn't want to live in a retirement village," he said. "I want to be around the children, close to life."

René was a gray-haired, bushy-browed man with owlish glasses and a long, elegantly straight nose. A half hour into our conversation, he rolled up a sleeve to show me the identification numbers that had been tattooed on his forearm at Auschwitz. I had expected ugly, ruthless scars. Instead I saw numerals, carefully inscribed, every seraph and flourish in place. The odds that René would survive even a few months in camp were slim, yet someone—a German? another Jew?—with an eye for beauty had executed his task with care.

René was born in Salonika, Greece, to a proud Turkish-speaking family that traced its ancestry to the aristocratic Sephardic Jews of medieval Spain. His father was the well-to-do owner of a flourishing export business. René's father, mother, and brother died at Auschwitz, but René survived to return to Salonika at the close of World War II. There, he married his childhood friend Tillie. The couple eventually migrated to the United States, where René worked in management for Sears, Roebuck & Co. and was active at Oakland's Temple Sinai.

Sorrow caught up with René again when the couple's only child, a son, died suddenly of a heart attack at age thirty-two. The final cruelty was the Oakland firestorm of 1991, which destroyed the Molhos' house and all their photographs of their son.

"I don't think my wife ever recovered," René said. "After that I quit my job and did nothing."

"What keeps you going then?"

René cast his eyes tenderly toward the upstairs room where Tillie had retreated when I arrived. "Sometimes at night I feel sad, no children or grandchildren. But my wife, I love her very much. It's important to be always happy—to make her happy."

René's story begins in the thriving, ancient Jewish community of Salonika. He tells it in a voice heavy with the Turkish accents of his youth.

René Molho—His Story

I lived an enchanted childhood. I was born in Salonika in 1919. My father was wealthy, and we were a close, loving Jewish family. We all lived in the same house, my mother and father, my grandparents, my younger brother, and I.

Then on my twenty-second birthday, April 9, 1941, the Germans occupied Salonika. Two years later, they put my parents and my brother and me on a train. They locked us in a cattle car, and took us to the concentration camp at Auschwitz-Birkenau in Poland. Right away they killed my parents, they sent them to the gas chambers, and my brother and I went into camp.

Four months later, my brother was selected for experiments on his testicles. They removed one testicle without anesthesia, and then the other, and they killed him that way. I was the only one in my family still alive after the war. I survived two-and-a-half years at Auschwitz-Birkenau, which is a record, I think.

My experience tells me that the same man can be bad one day and good the next. Sometimes I am good, at other times, I act badly. Nobody is perfect, nobody is Mother Teresa. I've done good things that I am proud of. And I've done one bad thing; and I cannot forget it.

I will tell you first about a good thing that I did. For about seven months at Auschwitz-Birkenau I had a very good work station. See, when the Jews came in on the trains to the camp, most of them went straight to the gas chamber, and they left all their belongings in the train. So there was a detail of prisoners, which I was in, who went and picked up all of the belongings. Of course, there was always some food in there, and we would steal the food and smuggle some into camp to give to people we knew.

We worked twelve-hour shifts—work twelve hours, relax and sleep eight hours, then work another twelve hours. Sometimes we

slept right there at work because there were so many people coming in on the trains. But usually we came back to camp at the end
of a shift. The guards lined us up in rows of five, counted us, and
searched us. If they caught a guy with food, they killed him.

It was pretty gutsy, but a lot of us smuggled the food in anyway. If we had extra food we stayed in the middle of a row, and
after they checked the row in front of us, we switched places with
a guy they just searched. We were all friends, like brothers, and
everybody in all the rows knew what everybody else was doing. I
don't know if I would do that again now. If the guards caught me,
they would kill me or beat me to death, one or the other. There is
an age difference; you don't act the same way when you are seventy-eight as you do when you are twenty-four. It was a daring thing
I did, but then I didn't care.

I don't think I am a bad person, but I've done bad things as
well as the good things. One thing in particular I am not proud
of. Near the end of the war, the Germans sent all of us from
Auschwitz back to Germany. The Russian troops were coming
and the Germans didn't want to leave any evidence behind. So
they burned the camp and the crematory, and they piled us all
into cattle trains, the same way we came in, but this time they
really packed us in.

In Germany, in a camp somewhere between Oranienburg and
Dachau, we were made to work all day carrying cement, two sacks
at a time, to the top of a flight of stairs. We were exhausted. Since
it was bitter cold, some of the prisoners insulated themselves with
the paper sacks, they stuffed the paper under their shirts, but if
they were caught, they were beaten. I did not take the risk of a
beating.

There was a prisoner who was dying, who was very sick. I didn't
have any shoes, and this for me was a matter of life and death. So

I stole his shoes. The guy was dying, and I took his shoes. He saw me as I did this, and to this day I cannot forget the expression on his face. I see it in many nightmares. Today, I am ashamed of that. I'm sure he died, I hope.

I did that one thing in my life and it bothers me. It haunts me. And that, not fasting and not lighting candles, is my penance. My own feelings, that is my punishment. Since I did that thing, I haven't injured anybody knowingly. I've tried not to. I don't know if God notices what I do, but I sure do.

13

"Do I Need Two Big Macs?"

Geoff and René convinced me that my choices matter, what I do matters. I can't know for sure what God is, if God is at all. But I can be and do and act the way I want the universe to be. From another of my interviewees, Dwight Dutschke, I learned a new way to think about my ethical choices. If I watch and listen and reflect on things, Dwight told me, if I quiet myself, nature and the world as it is will show me what to do.

The drive from Oakland up to Dwight's farmhouse near Ione in California's Gold Country was a long one: A rush of suburban freeways, a curving two-laner through farmland studded with grape vines and walnut trees, then the town of Ione. Known variously as Bedbug and Freezeout during Gold Rush times, on the day I visited Ione it was still a small town with two-story shops and façade roofs contemplating one other across a narrow Main Street.

Dwight had suggested we meet on a street corner in the center of town, so I found myself standing on the sidewalk waiting for him on a sunny February day, feeling conspicuously the out-of-towner. My discomfort quickly evaporated, however, as a sturdily built man with short legs and wide shoulders approached me on the sidewalk, hand extended. It was Dwight. His dark eyes lit up with pleasure as he shook my hand. I climbed back into my station wagon and followed Dwight's car out of town onto a country road. After a series of confounding left and right turns onto one bumpy country road after another, we arrived at last at the farmhouse that had once belonged to Dwight's maternal great-grandparents.

Dwight's family had lived in these rolling Sierra Nevada foothills for generations. The German and Danish ranchers on his father's side had been here a century, running dairy cattle on the fertile grasslands. His mother's family, Miwok Indians, had been here much longer.

We entered the farmhouse through the kitchen door. The house was old, but the kitchen was fresh and newly remodeled. On an island countertop at the center of the room, a huge rack of ribs simmered in an oversized slow cooker. Everyone in this family works, Dwight explained. His wife, his son, his daughter. The ribs would be just ready when people showed up for dinner.

A few days earlier, I had telephoned Dwight in Sacramento, at the California Office of Historic Preservation where he worked, to finalize this appointment. As we talked, I noticed that I barely gave him time to respond to one question before I had moved on to the next. Slow down, I told myself, this is not the kind of person who scrambles from thought to thought. And sure enough, when we finally sat down at the kitchen table to talk, the point that Dwight was to make that day was—you can have too many questions, you can be in too much of a hurry. Listen to the woodpecker; it will tell you its name. Slow down with the questions, or you might miss the answers.

Dwight Dutschke—His Story

Up in the Sierra Nevada foothills, off highway 88, there's a little valley with meadows and oak trees and a big outcropping of marbleized limestone where the local Native Americans used to grind acorns. You can still see the holes they made in that rock, hundreds of them. The deeper holes were used to crack the shells of the acorns, the shallower holes to grind the meat. Whenever a hole got too deep, they'd start another one next to it.

The place is called Chaw'se, which means grinding rock in the Northern Miwok language. The state made it into a park in 1968, Indian Grinding Rock State Historic Park, and I went to work there right out of college. The people who worked at the park at the time wanted to know more about the Indian culture, and since my family on my mother's side was Miwok, they kept asking me questions. There was a ball field at Chaw'se, for example, where the Indians used to play Indian football. The people at work wanted to know the Miwok word for ball field so they could put up a sign with the correct name on it. I wanted to know too, because I had my own questions about my Indian ancestors, a lot of them.

My father's family, the Dutschkes, were German and Danish dairy ranchers. They go back a hundred years around here but, of course, compared to my mother's family they're newcomers. They were Methodists, and when I got to be about five, the Methodism kicked in pretty good, and for the next ten years or so, Mom was taking me and my three sisters to church on a regular basis. I was aware of Native American religion at the time, but I didn't do much with it.

I was fortunate growing up, because I got to spend a lot of time with the old people on my mother's side. They were Plains Miwok and Northern Miwok. My great-grandfather was Northern Miwok and he was one of the people who sued the federal government in the 1920s and again in the 1950s in the California Indians lands claims case. His son, my grandfather, was a singer who used to sing for the dances at the big Indian gatherings all around the region, and as a little kid I picked up a lot just by going places with him.

My family, what they wanted me to do was survive. My grandmother on my mother's side thought I should go ahead and become a part of the dominant society. "It's all good and well, being traditional," she said. "But you need to make a living." So I did all the things they wanted me to do. I went to school and to church and to college. I studied agriculture at Cal State Fresno, but while I was there I took a bunch of Native American studies classes, which probably helped me get the job at the state park.

I hadn't been working long at Chaw'se before I had collected a big list of questions about the Miwok people, some mine, some from the park rangers, starting with what we could put on that sign up by the ball field. One day after work, I drove over to see my grandmother and great-grandmother and I took my list with me.

My grandmothers lived over near Ione, where I grew up. They had houses, simple wood frame and painted white, right next to each other on a two-and-a-half-acre parcel with a creek running through it. They were seventy-something and ninety-something years old at the time. Both my grandmother and my great-grandmother had been informants back in the 1920s for famous anthropologists like Samuel A. Barrett. There were whole books full of Miwok culture and language sitting in the library at the University of California, Berkeley that my great-grandmother had been one of the main sources for. She was one of the few people still alive at the time who still lived the old culture and knew the language.

When I drove over to see my grandmothers that day, there wasn't a question I could ask them that they hadn't been asked fifty times, but I didn't know that yet. I was young. I wanted to know everything, and I wanted to know it all yesterday. We sat down around the maple dining room table in my grandmother's house. It seated four and it was new probably. My grandmother liked new things.

I took out my list. "Grandma and Great-Grandma," I said. "Can you tell me the Miwok word for the ball field up there at Chaw'se?"

"It has no name."

"Well, then. How would you say 'where they play ball'?"

My grandmothers took their time answering. They were quiet, calm ladies. Short, medium built, with glasses and neat, grey hair. They always dressed in dresses with hems down below the knees. They looked like Indians, no doubt about that. Probably looked like me. And they had worked all their lives, taking care of people's houses, taking care of people's children, working in the fields, cutting and picking hops, picking walnuts. They did hard work as well, loading clay into train cars by hand. They knew what a good day's work was.

"Well," my grandmother said finally. "If you want to say 'where they play ball,' I can tell you that. It's *poscoi-awea*."

"Yes. That's it," said my great-grandmother. "*Poscoi-awea*."

I said the words over and over to myself. *Poscoi-awea. Poscoi-awea*. I wasn't good at languages, I'm still not, and I didn't want to forget. Later, back at the park somebody listened to me repeat the words and wrote them out phonetically. *Poscoi-awea*. And that's how the sign at the ball field reads to this day.

I went back to talk to my grandmother and great-grandmother pretty often after that. This went on for a few years. I'd arrive with my list of questions, and sometimes they'd be too tired or not interested. But usually they'd say, "Okay, let's go through them." Though they'd heard the questions before, there I was, twenty-five years old, and in their eyes I could do no wrong. So they'd humor me. "Oh," they'd say. "Now *that's* an interesting question."

I was driven. I was afraid that my grandmother, my great-grandmother, and the things they knew were the last vestiges of a culture, my culture, that was becoming extinct. That's the way anthropologists and historians think of it. If we don't save it now, it's going to drop off the face of the earth. And that does happen, of course; cultures live and they die. But later on, as I got older, I realized that just my participating in the culture keeps it alive. I don't have to know the answers to all the questions. I don't have to remember the Miwok names of all the different woodpeckers.

But back then I thought, gee whiz, if I don't learn it from them now, how am I ever going to learn it? I had learned about Christianity in church, but Native American religion? There'd been no Sunday school for that. I asked them about everything from material culture—how do you trap a quail?—to the more philosophical questions—what happens after death? Sometimes it would take them a while to come up with an answer.

One time, out of the blue, my grandmother said a Miwok word to me.

"Huh?" I said. I didn't know why she was telling me this word, and right now I can't even remember what the word was.

She said the word again. "It means eagle. The other day, you wanted to know the word for eagle."

It had taken her three days to come up with it, but she did.

In high school I'd had an English teacher who was teaching us twelfth-century poetry. He said English wasn't spoken as quickly back then as it is now; they spoke fewer syllables per minute. He wanted us to read the old poetry out loud, and slow ourselves way down. It flows better that way. It's the same with Indian culture. In the old times, they didn't have to be home at five and have dinner done by six so they could be to a meeting at seven. They didn't have to rush through things, so the pace of conversation was different. More like a waltz than a foxtrot.

Finally I realized that these old people were like poetry. I had to slow myself down when I was with them. I was too energetic, I wanted to know it all today, I was wearing them out, and what they wanted me to do was to think about things. Often I'd ask a question, and they'd just ask me a question back. Now I see they wanted to gauge the maturity of my understanding before they gave me an answer.

When I asked them, "Why does the door of the roundhouse face east?" they just said, "Why do you think it faces east?"

"I don't know."

"When do you dance?"

"You dance at night."

"Well, if the door faces east, what happens when the sun comes up?"

"It shines through the door."

"Yes. It shines light into the roundhouse and then you know to quit dancing."

They could tell me things like that. They could tell me how they ground the acorns and how they used a certain tool. They could give me the names of all the plants. But if I asked them a spiritual question, they would say, "How can I tell you about that, if you've never had the experience yourself?"

Once I asked, "Why are there four poles in the round house?"

"Why do you think there are four poles in the round house?

"I don't know. Tell me."

"How many directions are there?"

"Four."

"How many seasons are there?"

"Four."

"Well, does nature do things in fours?"

"Yes."

That was the answer, nature does things in fours. It's a perfectly satisfactory answer, and you can go over to the UC-Berkeley library, read Barrett, and get the same answer. If kids ask me about the four poles, that's what I tell them.

But my grandmother and great-grandmother wanted me to explore for myself and find the deeper answer. It wasn't something they could teach me. They could only give me the framework, or a clue. The experience had to be my own. When they said, "Nature does things in fours," I think they were telling me to look for the answer in nature. The answer was completely natural and simple, but I would have to understand that for myself.

Later on, when I was working in the California Office of Historic Preservation, I tried to talk with my grandmother about what the tradition would say about reburying human remains. At the time, whenever archaeologists or construction workers came across the graves of Native Americans, the state would take the remains and curate them—put them in museums. One warehouse in Sacramento had the remains of about nine hundred people stored in it. Today it's fairly common practice for remains like that to be returned to the local tribe for reburial, but at that time there was a lot of opposition to reburial from archaeologists and other scientists. I was one of the people making the case for reburial, but I didn't know how that could be done respectfully, so I went to my grandmothers to find out.

"What if somebody was buried in the ground and you had to dig them up and move them," I said. "What kind of ceremony would you do?"

"We would never dig them up and move them."

"But what if you had to move them, would you do a song? Would you do a ceremony?"

"We wouldn't move them."

They couldn't answer my question. It was completely outside their frame of thought. It was a foreign concept. I noticed that the same thing was true for me when they talked about the old-time medicine men and doctoring. I had no frame of reference. They could tell me the details, but I had no means of understanding any of it because I'd had none of those experiences myself.

But I was young and I had to ask my questions. I thought that was the way I was going to learn. I was going to ask all these questions, and they were going to magically give me the answers, just like in school. Anyway, my great-grandmother finally put it to me. "If you have to ask the question," she said, "you probably won't get the answer. You have to let the answer come to you."

When I stopped framing my questions in modern Western terms and I became more open to the things around me, more observant and reflective, I found that she was right; messages came to me all the time. And that's the lesson I most remember of everything I learned from my grandmother and great-grandmother, to be reflective. Do I remember the word for eagle? No, I don't. But I do remember that one thing, which they really couldn't teach me.

That's why the high places are so important to some Native American groups. You go up the mountain to slow down and to think. It's quiet up there. No one is yapping in your ear or telling you to go and gather something so you can eat. You wander up this hill, you find a rock to sit on, you fast a little, you look out, and it's the world as you know it, your whole world for maybe forty miles around, probably the distance you might travel in your entire lifetime. Everything you need to survive is within sight of that mountaintop. It's the world that Creator has made for you and left for you to manage and conserve. It's the world that makes you a living and allows your children to grow up.

At Mount Shasta, in Northern California, there is this place called Creator's Seat, an indentation in the side of the mountain where God or Creator or however you describe him sits and reflects on what he has done. He wants you to do the same. Slow down. And as you look over the world, you see what your role is out there. You decide maybe you have gone too far in one direction. Maybe you have been too positive, accumulating too many things. Or maybe you have been too negative, not looking at things in a positive enough light. You weigh your needs against the needs of other people. You try to get a balance.

For years when I was a kid I'd hear these old guys, these Indian people, say they needed to go up to the mountains to get their power. But in my feeble understanding, I thought they were going up there to get their batteries recharged so they could work better, or get a knee up on things. Back then, I wanted to control things, to make things better for myself, and to acquire material things. But now after some sitting and reflecting, and not asking so darned many questions, my thinking is just the opposite. Now I ask how am I going to interact with the world so as to minimally affect it?

During the 1970s I worked with a real famous basket weaver up in Washington. With some groups it's not respectful to say their names after they have passed away, so I won't mention hers. One of the things this weaver taught me was that, when I went out to gather sedge root to make a basket, I had no right to take all the sedge root I found. If the root was three feet long, I should take only two feet, so that the plant has something to start over with.

So I guess religion as I practice it is going up the side of that mountain and thinking about how I am going to interact with the world as I know it. There is no such thing as correct or right. I don't need a goal at the end. The goal at the end is that I am going to die. The question is how will I continue on my journey? Do I really need a particular thing or don't I? Do I really want two McDonald's burgers? Do I need one at all? Should I take it or leave it there? That is my religious philosophy. Reflectiveness.

I once knew this old Indian lady named Marie Potts. She looked a lot like my grandmother and great-grandmother. Small, quiet, calm, wore glasses, worked all her life. And she was pretty famous. She started an Indian newspaper, *Smoke Signals*, and was a big advocate for Indian rights. Sometimes she'd lead nature walks for groups of people.

One day on one of these outings—a friend told me this story— Marie is walking and talking about the world and her beliefs in life, and this little boy picks up a rock and throws it.

Marie stops talking and says to the boy, "Ah! What gave you the right to change the direction of that rock?"

And the little boy looks at her, puzzled.

And Marie says, "Well, it took thousands and thousands of years for that rock to get to where it was. That was its journey. And then you picked it up and changed its entire direction. What gave you the right to do that without thinking about it?"

It's a story I still think about. I've thrown enough rocks in my life. It's not that you shouldn't throw the rock. It's just that you should be aware that if you do, you are making a difference. You don't do things just because you can. Or because you think you need to. You do things because, after you have sat down and thought about it, it's the right thing to do.

No matter what you do you will interrupt the flow of the world. That's the nature of your survival. But every once in a while you need to sit still and reflect on things. Like when you are interviewing old people, slowing down so that you don't just run past them. So that you actually know when you've got there.

PART SIX: *Finding God
in a Close Community*

14

Serving the Dead

If you've gotten this far in this book you know that, since childhood, I've thought of God as a mighty personage, a metaphysical entity who is *out there somewhere*. A being who is not of this world, who is all-knowing and all-powerful. Which is why I am intrigued by people who aren't much interested in the Big Guy Up in the Sky. What makes these people tick, I wonder? What drives them? Susan Lefelstein strikes me as one such person. Like so many of the humanitarians I've encountered in my journey as a religion writer, Susan is more interested in the people around her than she is in speculating on the nature of God.

Susan's passion, her sense of the sacred, is located very much in the here and now, and specifically in the here and now of her Jewish community. It's people she cares about, Jewish people, the Jews of her New York upbringing—the kosher butcher down the street, the rabbis, the synagogues every few blocks, the neighbors, the relatives, the friends—and, now that she lives and works in California, the Jews of the San Francisco Bay Area. It's a community that's diluted and spread over several counties, but a community nonetheless.

Susan is retired now, but at the time of our first conversation, she found her spiritual practice in the down-to-earth work of preparing the bodies of her fellow Jews for burial. It was human beings that Susan felt called to serve, the bereaved family members who came to her mortuary for help as well as their deceased loved ones, now mute and helpless. Her profession allowed Susan to find God not so much in the transcendent as in the earthly images of God, living and dead. This is how she described her work to me.

Susan Lefelstein—Her Story

I'm the director of Sinai Memorial Chapel, a Jewish Mortuary in Lafayette. We work only with Jewish families. We're a non-profit organization and all our profits at the end of the year are given out in grants to various Jewish schools, programs, and organizations. So one of the nice things about working for Sinai is that we do a lot of good.

Working for a Jewish mortuary, I come in contact with many people who have gotten away from the religion or who were not brought up as involved in the religion as their elders. Now they're making arrangements for grandparents or parents, and they want to do the right thing. I'm able to tell them what the tradition is and help them do their family members that final honor. Being able to help people is a very special thing. It's hard to work with death day in and day out; and certainly when children die, it's very, very upsetting to us. People are in the worst part of their lives when they come to us, but I can help them with the process and that makes my job gratifying.

Judaism outlines a specific preparation of a body for burial—prayers, washing, dressing, casketing. It's done by a mostly volunteer group called the *chevra kadisha*, or "holy burial society." The *chevra kadisha* tradition traces itself back all the way to the time of Moses. When Moses died, in a cave, God tended to him personally and prepared his body. The preparation is called *tahara*, and it's a very loving, very respectful process. The body must be prepared by Jewish people who have been trained, so that a non-Jew doesn't prepare a Jew for burial. Only women can prepare a woman. Only men can prepare a man. During the preparation you never talk about anything but the preparation. You never turn your back on the body. We treat the body as we would our Torah, our holy books, and we believe that a person is made in the image of God.

The Jewish religion prescribes a format for the prayers, for when to wash, how to wash, and what clothing to put on. The first washing is strictly a washing, just to cleanse the body. The second is a pouring of water, twenty-four quarts poured continuously, without stopping, which is a symbolic purification. We're purifying this body to meet God. Symbolically? Who knows? We pray for God to protect the soul. Then the body is dressed in shrouds and placed in the casket. Earth from Israel is placed in the casket to symbolize that this person has been buried in the Holy Land, which for us, of course, is Israel.

When the person is dressed in traditional shrouds and placed in the casket, there's a sense of peace, a look of peace that comes over the person that you can't explain, but you know you've been part of some unexplainable transition. And you've done a very good deed. You've done something that nobody's going to say thank you for, and you're not getting paid for, but you've done something very special for this person. And, hopefully, someone will do it for me some day.

Sometimes a "watcher" sits with the body to protect the soul until burial—rest. Mostly only the Orthodox do this now. The watcher sits and reads from the Book of Psalms, from the time of death till the time of burial. In many cases families themselves will come in and sit with the body. They "don't want Mother to be left alone." We use wood caskets with no metal or nails, because metal and nail do not break down as quickly in the ground. We're supposed to go back to the earth in a natural state. No embalming, because that's a preservative, and it doesn't do anything for the dead. Basically it just preserves the body for viewing by the living. The more quickly we bury the body, the more honor and respect for the dead. I mean there's a person lying there that can't do anything for themselves; it's the shell of the person that's no longer needed. And so the more respect is to bury quickly.

The Jewish religion is based on many things, of course, but helping others, that's one of the all-time important things. Being able to help mourners, being able to help people who don't have enough money, doing acts of loving kindness for others who are less fortunate is a great mitzvah, a good deed, and that makes me feel very good.

15

"Put Me In, Coach!"

Stace Hall is a true believer. He believes in God. He believes in family. He believes in friendship. And he believes ardently in his church and its leadership. He is a Mormon, a member of the Church of Jesus Christ of Latter-day Saints. And like Susan Lefelstein, he is very much a part of his community.

The LDS church is huge, thirteen million members worldwide. But it runs a tight ship. Mormon temples and rituals are sacred—and off limits to anyone but members in good standing. To maintain that standing, members must meet regularly with a church official to examine their spiritual and personal lives. In many ways, it's a closed society. And though the church values community service, much of its charitable efforts are directed, not outward to the larger community, but inward to church members.

For some people, including me, so much scrutiny and togetherness would make for a claustrophobic environment. Not for Stace. He thrives on the intense personal interconnectedness of Mormon culture and theology. He believes in giving his all to his church and its projects. After much study and prayer to reach a personal conviction—or as Stace calls it, a testimony—regarding church doctrine, he accedes to his church's teachings and to its earthly authority over him.

When I first talked to Stace, he seemed so vulnerable, his faith in God so ebullient and unguarded, that I worried about him. But after spending some time in Salt Lake City with Stace and other LDS church members during a Religion Newswriters Association conference, it became clear to me that the Mormon culture has built and maintains its own particular version of reality. It values young men like Stace. The vast, worldwide LDS network takes care of its own. And this loveable young man is definitely one of its own.

I met Stace through Kim Farah, a public relations officer at the LDS headquarters in Salt Lake City. Young LDS males are encouraged to devote two years to missionary service, and Kim put me in touch with several brand-new veterans of the program. Stace's story stood out. In the second year of his missionary service, thousands of miles from home, he fell ill. Though he was in intensive care, his parents were not permitted—by church policy—to go to his bedside.

Stace and I agreed to meet in the lobby of my hotel on a Sunday afternoon. I arrived early, settled into an easy chair, and lost myself in a magazine. Minutes later, out of the corner of my eye, I saw what looked like a middle-aged businessman in a dark suit coming toward me across the lobby.

"You must be Barbara."

I looked up. The businessman was actually a blond, pink-cheeked youth, walking toward me with an uneven gait, his suit two sizes too big. Stace and I shook hands and we made our way to the hotel restaurant for a lunch that lasted nearly till dinnertime. Stace's stomach was bothering him just a little that day, so he told his story between carefully chewed bites.

Stace Hall—His Story

I had wanted to be a missionary for the Church of Jesus Christ of Latter-day Saints for as long as I could remember. When I was little, church missionaries would come to dinner at my family's house in Vernal, in northeastern Utah. They were young guys, nineteen, twenty years old, and they all followed the LDS missionary dress code: the short haircut, the white shirt, the tie. They came from all over the world to do mission work in our area, and my mom, who's a fourth-generation Latter-day Saint, would break out the fine china and cook a nice dinner for them. One missionary, I remember, was a professional soccer player from Brazil. Another had a really cool handshake; he kind of twisted his hand around yours and gave you a thumbs-up at the end. I wanted to be like that guy.

Some people wondered whether I could serve effectively as a missionary. I was born three months early with circulation problems. My feet turned black and some of my toes fell off. The doctors gave me a 10 percent, then a 0 percent, chance to live. But I made it through, and now I play golf and basketball without any problems. My feet are a little bit fragile and I wear like a three-inch lift on my left shoe, but I don't let any of it stop me. It's just part of who I am and nothing a good resurrection won't fix.

As soon as I was old enough, nineteen, I applied to the Office of the First Presidency of the LDS Church to be a missionary. I was away at college at the time, a freshman at Brigham Young University, and the letter from the President's Office came in the mail to our house in Vernal. I was so excited, I couldn't wait to see what it said, so I drove all the way home from college just to open the envelope. When I got there, everyone in my family clamored around to watch—my mom, my little sister, and my little brother beside me on the couch, and my dad across the room with the video camera. I opened the envelope, and sure enough, it was my missionary call.

"Dear Elder Hall, You have been recommended as one worthy to represent the Lord Jesus Christ. You are hereby called to labor in the Pennsylvania Philadelphia mission . . . You will report to the Missionary Training Center in Provo, Utah, on April 30 . . . "

Sweet! Put me in, coach. I'm here in full readiness.

My dad owned a trucking business at the time, and when April 30 came around, the whole family drove the hundred and fifty miles to Provo in one of his trucks, a Ford Dualie, my dear mom sobbing most of the way. There was a reception for new missionaries at the center, and some of my friends from BYU came up to say bye. The guys hugged me, but girls are asked not to hug male missionaries, so they just shook my hand. When it was time for my family to leave, it hit me like a ton of bricks. I wouldn't be seeing them again for two years. I wouldn't be allowed to leave the mission field during my mission, and my family wouldn't be allowed to visit. I could phone home twice a year only, on Christmas and Mother's Day. I cried, but I was resolute. I had a group hug with my family and I walked through the door to the training center.

LDS missionaries have a lot of constraints on them. No television. No movies. No dating. No going out with friends. Music—I'm a fan of soft rock, Phil Collins, and Bruce Hornsby—but we were allowed uplifting music only, mostly church music. We could write letters one day of the week, on preparation day, but if you got a letter, you didn't have to wait. You could read it right away, which was good, because I craved those letters. Male missionaries wear a suit every day, and if it's hot, just a shirt, tie, and dress pants. My parents bought me this suit I'm wearing today for my mission. It's dark gray pinstripe to fit in back east.

In the mission field, the mission president is your leader and your guide. He assigns you to a mission area and to a mission companion, and he watches over you. On hot days, he's the one who tells you whether or not a suit coat is required. My mission president was Joseph Cook from Salt Lake City. My first assignment was to Smyrna, Delaware, and my first mission companion was Elder Clay Broadhead from Afton, Wyoming, which was way neat, because I was really into sports and Elder Broadhead had been an all-conference and all-state basketball player in high school.

During your mission, you're with your companion missionary twenty-four-seven. You share an apartment, you eat together, you work together, and you study together. You're never alone, except to shower or use the bathroom. Elder Broadhead and I ate most of our dinners in restaurants or at the houses of local LDS members. The members loved to feed us the same way my mom fed the missionaries in Vernal. And that was way nice, because if I was cooking, it was noodle soup or peanut butter sandwiches.

I had several different mission companions over the months. Besides Elder Broadhead, there was Elder Dennis Torres from Henderson, Nevada, and Elder Rue Larsen from Brigham City, Utah. Whoever I was with, we kept to a strict schedule. Up every day at six-thirty to study scripture. Work from nine-thirty a.m. to nine-thirty p.m. In bed by ten-thirty. As part of our work, we might deliver a copy of the Book of Mormon or the Bible to someone who'd seen an ad on TV, or we'd visit LDS members that we hadn't seen at church to let them know we cared. We did a lot of service work: Grocery shopping for an elderly woman in Allentown. Helping LDS families build a fence or remodel their home.

We'd go door-to-door quite a bit, trying to talk to people. We didn't have a lot of success with that. On a hot day, people might let us in and give us lemonade or water, but they didn't want to hear what we had to say. The Pennsylvania winters were as cold and humid as the summers were hot, and that cold cut right to the bone. We had to bundle up so much we looked like sumo wrestlers. Our hands got so cold and stiff it hurt to knock. After a while, we started taking along a golf ball to do the knocking. We'd go to maybe thirty doors in a day, and every third day we'd actually get to talk with someone about what we believed. It was disheartening, because I felt then and feel now that we had the most important message anyone could be given, and people were turning us away. Nevertheless, we kept going.

Later, knocking doors, or "tracting," was my favorite thing to do. Pick a neighborhood, and go. You always had a surprise. In Smyrna, a lady came out on her porch, looked us up and down, and said, "God gave you boys two handsome bodies, why are you out wasting them?"

"Because we have something important to talk to you about," I said.

"And what would that be?"

"Your salvation."

"Well, I'm not interested." And she went back inside and slammed the door.

Once, Elder Torres and I were knocking doors in Catasauqua, Pennsylvania, when a beautiful girl our age answered her door wearing nothing but a towel.

My first thought was, boy, I hope she keeps that towel on. Then I thought, I have a job to do here. She's a cute girl, no question, but I've got to maintain my focus. President Cook always said to look to heaven for guidance in the mission field. So that's what I did. I looked straight up at the sky.

"Can we come back when you're dressed?" I said, keeping my eyes averted heavenward.

"Sure."

Later, we went back to her house and stood outside her door in our ties and white shirts, gripping our scripture bags full of Bibles and copies of the Book of Mormon. We knocked, but she didn't come to the door. We weren't surprised. We were used to it by now.

One Saturday, about fifteen months into my mission, I woke up with immense pain in my left side. We were going to do service work for a local LDS family that day, yard work, and I told myself, suck it up, you'll be fine. When we got there I tried to pick up this concrete slab. I do dumb things sometimes, and this was one of them. The next thing I knew I was in a hospital gown going in for surgery. It turned out I had acute appendicitis—on the wrong side. Crazy.

When I woke up the next morning, standing in front of me were President Cook, Mrs. Cook, and two of the young missionaries from the district, asking me how I felt. It was great to visit with those folks, but then they left and I took a turn for the worse: I aspirated stomach acid into my lungs. The doctors were worried about pneumonia. They were going to send me down to the intensive care unit.

Mission rules are such that my mother and father couldn't come to Pennsylvania to visit me in the hospital. But President Cook kept them informed, and in his wisdom and inspiration, he told them that for as long as I was in the hospital it'd be fine for them to talk to me on the phone as often as they wanted. My parents were okay with that. But when they found out I was going into intensive care, they were ready to buy plane tickets. President Cook had to use his best public relations skills on them, especially my mom. He assured her everything would be okay; he'd make sure I was looked after.

Getting wheeled down to intensive care was like plunging into a hole. It was horrible down there. The rest of the hospital was brightly colored and cheery feeling. But down there it was bleak and sad. Dark. No windows. Even the staff people looked sad. I was put in this dreary room by myself, this bat cave, and I had a nurse, bless her heart, who told me I smelled bad and needed deodorant. I was in immense pain and was hooked up to an IV and some kind of monitor that was attached to the wall. But when I asked this nurse for a pillow from the other side of the room, she told me to get up and get it myself.

I'm not sure how long I was alone in that ICU room. It felt like days. The minutes ticked by about as fast as a boulder just sitting there. I had nothing to look forward to. The missionaries came by, but they couldn't stay forever, and it got to be really, really lonely. It seemed no one cared, no one was aware of me or my situation. I was in a bed in the middle of nowhere.

Then I remembered God. I thought, how foolish of me to think that I'm alone. I need to pray for some help. "Heavenly Father," I said. "I really would appreciate something positive happening right now. I'm alone, and I'm at my wits' end. So if Thou would please send me something, I'd be so grateful. In the name of Jesus Christ, amen."

Right then I noticed this other nurse sitting at a desk out in the hall. She was a heavy-set lady, about thirty-five, and jolly acting. When she saw me looking at her she came walking into the room.

"I've noticed something about you," she said. "Something different."

"I'm a missionary of the Church of Jesus Christ of Latter-day Saints."

"Oh, really? I've heard of that church. What do you guys believe?"

Now this was way neat. This lady was going to give me a chance to talk about the things I hold dear.

"Well," I said. "I know for a fact that God knows you, and knows who you are, and knows you by name."

"Oh!" she said, taking a big deep breath.

I told her about the prophets. Noah, Abraham, Moses, and the ultimate prophet—Jesus Christ, the literal Son of God, the Savior.

She was looking at me with such intensity, taking it all in. So I kept going. I told her about Joseph Smith and the LDS Church. And it was beautiful. Here I was in this dreary, icky, windowless hole, hooked up to an IV and feeling down in the dumps, but I was getting to give the testimony I'd been trying to give for months. It was almost poetic how majestic it was in that dungeon right then.

We talked like this for ten or fifteen minutes, and she was getting teary. Pretty soon it was time for her to go back to work, so I gave her a copy of the Book of Mormon and she left the room.

When she was gone, I said, "Thanks, Heavenly Father. I needed that."

It was killing me, just stewing there in a hospital bed, so when I finally got out I rushed things a bit. Two weeks after I left the hospital, I helped some LDS members move a couch up from their cellar, which may have had some residual effects later on, because today I still have some stomach pains. But so what? No big deal. I wouldn't trade it. The mission experience was everything I'd wanted times a million. I was able to serve others, and I hope my service is acceptable to Heavenly Father, because I gave it everything I had.

A few months after the surgery, it became obvious that I couldn't keep up with the mission work. I kept running out of gas.

I needed to go home to get some rest and some medical care. And so, after eighteen months in the mission field, six months before my mission was supposed to be over, my time as a full-time missionary came to a close. It was time to go home.

My plane rolled over the Rockies into Utah, a gorgeous sight, like no other. Ah, I had missed those mountains. In Salt Lake I got the first sight of my parents in baggage claim, and they got their first sight of me. I had lost probably twenty-five pounds, and the pinstriped suit was baggy on me. But they were thrilled, because they knew I had given it my all. I hugged my mom first, then my dad. And we just stood there underneath the scrolling sign, crying.

It was a huge priority to have my parents be proud of me, but even more important to have my Heavenly Father be pleased with me. Heavenly Father is the ultimate parent, friend, and leader. And he wants to hear from his children. That's what I think is neat. This perfect Being, who created me and created you and is beyond comprehension, wants a twenty-year-old mortal to approach him in prayer. He wants to hear from me when I study for a test, or when I'm at my wits' end on a hospital bed in the bat cave. Isn't that marvelous? It makes me love him all the more.

PART SEVEN: *Ancestral Wisdom*

16

The Nun's Daughter

On a spring evening in Lent, I settled into a pew to hear Huston Smith, the popular religion scholar and author of the best-selling *The World's Religions*, speak to the question: what can the world's religious traditions learn from each other? It was part of a lecture series hosted by St. Stephen's Episcopal Church in Orinda, not too far from my house. The church was crowded with hundreds of expectant listeners. I was covering religion for the *Contra Costa Times* at the time, but I wasn't here on assignment. I was here to expand my spiritual horizons. I'd driven through the Caldecott Tunnel from home, hoping to get a glimpse of God that I wasn't getting in my not-so-regular Sunday morning trips to my little church in Oakland.

The question was a provocative one. What can the wisdom traditions of the world teach each other? Smith had written and rewritten the book on the subject. Born in 1919 in China to Methodist missionary parents and now a visiting professor emeritus of religious studies at the University of California, Berkeley, Smith had studied world religions for most of his life.

Studied? Not really. Huston Smith had *lived* the world's great religions. In his book *Tales of Wonder* he reveals that he "practiced Hinduism unconditionally for ten years, then Buddhism for ten years, and then Islam for another ten years—all the while remaining a Christian and regularly attending a Methodist church." If anyone knew something about the world's many wisdom traditions, it was Huston Smith. I wanted to know what he knew. What could the religions of the world teach each other? What could they teach me? Might there be a tradition out there somewhere that suits me better than the Christianity of my childhood? I was all ears.

Smith's answer took my breath away. It was—nothing.

"Each revelation is complete in itself," he told his audience. None of them lacks anything. None needs to borrow from the faith, practice, theology, or sacred texts of another.

Indeed, Smith believes that the cafeteria-style spirituality so popular today is risky. It allows the individual to pick and choose. And, spurred on and blinded by ego, the individual will not always choose wisely between Taoist apples and Kabbalist oranges. Better to submit to the discipline of a single wisdom tradition. Let it batter the ego, shape it, and sanctify it. After all, "We wouldn't be setting out on a spiritual path if our ego was already wise."

Of course, not everyone departs his or her religion of birth for theoretical reasons. Salma Arastu, a Berkeley painter who was born and raised in a devout Hindu family in India, fell in love with a Muslim architect while an art student in Hyderabad during the 1970s. "When I found out he was a Muslim," she told me during a visit to her painting studio, "I told myself, obviously this thing cannot happen. But I was in tears, because I really liked him."

The young Salma took her dilemma to Lord Krishna. Kneeling and crying in front of the household image of the deity, she said, "What is happening? What should I do?"

Each time she asked, she got the same response: "It's God's

permission. Why are you worrying?"

To keep the peace in her husband's family, Salma converted to Islam. "I didn't know anything about Islam," she said. "Nothing. I didn't even try to read about it. I didn't have that kind of mind. I felt, the rituals will change, but God is not going to change. He has promised me he's coming with me. So one day I just took the step; I went to my husband's house, I accepted Islam in the morning, and we were married that evening."

Later Salma had a chance to learn more about her adopted religion. "I found beauty and beauty and beauty—which is the real inspiration for my work. My paintings flow from my heart to my hand, from my God to my hand. I'm just a tool." Many of her paintings feature Arabic calligraphy and passages from the Qur'an, and Salma feels that God might have had a reason for lifting her from Hinduism to Islam: "My painting—I think this is it."

Since that evening at St. Stephen's Church listening to Huston Smith, I've met many ardent believers like Salma and experienced dozens of different faiths and denominations up close. I've learned from them. I've been stunned by their beauty. But over the years I've stuck to the religion of my birth, partly because Smith's advice makes so much sense to me and partly because the imagery of my childhood religion continues to hold me: Jesus washing the feet of his disciples the night before he died; Jesus welcoming children, women, tax collectors, and criminals to his side; Jesus restoring a blind man's sight with mud and spit.

Some of my most articulate and passionate interviewees are converts. Salma is one. Martin Verhoeven, a Buddhist teacher whose story appears later, is another. But others I've met along the way have stayed close to the faith of their fathers and mothers. Stace Hall was inspired to become a missionary by his parents' Mormon hospitality. Orenzia Bernstine was the son of an itiner-

ant Southern preacher. Dwight Dutschke's grandmothers lived
the spiritual traditions of their Miwok Indian ancestors. And the
person you'll hear from next, psychotherapist Savitri Hari, is the
daughter of a South Indian Hindu nun. All four—Savitri, Dwight,
Orenzia, and Stace—were born and reared in very different parts
of the world and in very different faith communities. Yet they have
something vital in common—families who were firmly grounded
in their respective traditions.

Like Salma, Savitri Hari is a first-generation American. She
and her husband live in a two-story stucco house on a cul-de-sac
in Walnut Creek. The Hari children are grown now, and the land-
scaped trees in the Haris' upscale suburban housing tract have
matured as well. One lawn blends into another here, uninterrupt-
ed by sidewalks or fences.

On the day of our first interview, Savitri sat on an upholstered
wingback chair in her large, carpeted living room. An Indian classical dancer as well as a psychotherapist, Savitri was in middle
age as trim and flexible as a teenager. She sat with her bare feet
resting happily on the chair's seat cushion, her knees wide apart,
and her spine upright and relaxed: She looked like a Hindu goddess in sweats. The red dot, the *bindi*, that many women of India
paint on their foreheads was missing; Savitri had parted with that
tradition years ago. On this day, her only ornament was a single
diamond stud piercing the curve of her right nostril.

As Savitri and I talked, I noticed myself watching as well as
listening. Savitri was a study in grace, but not a western sort of
grace. That was for me to attempt from where I sat on a nearby
sofa. As a first-time guest in this house, I was sitting as I had been
taught to sit as a girl growing up in the Midwest. Feet on the floor,
knees together, hands in my lap, elbows at my sides.

My hostess had sat on cushions and floors as a child. I had

spent my girlhood in chairs—sofas, pews, bleachers, the bucket seats of convertibles. Sitting here now with Savitri, minding my manners, knees, and elbows, I realized that for much of my life, I have been uncomfortable. When I keep my knees together like this, my spine rolls back, my shoulders round, and my chin juts forward. I could learn something, I thought, by paying attention to how Savitri lives in her body.

Savitri went into the kitchen to squeeze oranges into juice, and I walked around the room, studying the pictures on the walls. They were of Indian classical dancers, large-breasted and full-buttocked, striking effortless poses. Their faces were serene, suggesting neither physical exertion nor shame at the astonishing sensuality of their bodies. Later I would learn that, for Savitri, dance is a spiritual practice as well as an art form. It's her sure connection to God. She has learned from her body that a divine energy courses through all of nature.

Over the years and through our many conversations, I have come to admire Savitri. She believes that her choices matter. She refuses to feel bitterness at the disappointments in her life, she allies herself daily with the forces of compassion and, although she is an intensely spiritual woman, she chooses not to escape into the life of the spirit. Instead, she embraces the voluptuous beauty of this world—her body, dance, nature, even the cow dung she shaped into mandalas as a child. And, finally, she has chosen to shape the ancient heritage she received from her family into something that sustains her in twenty-first-century America.

Savitri returned with the orange juice and continued her story. Her childhood had been a sad one, I learned. Before she was born, a simple thing—a piece of rice stalk—had changed the course of her life and deprived her of her father and of the full measure of her mother's love. As she spoke, Savitri's hands drew graceful shapes in the air and her voice rose and fell with the rhythms of Telugu, the musical language of South India.

Savitri Hari—Her Story

My father was working in a field on his family's land in Andhrapradesh, South India, when a piece of rice stalk got stuck in his foot. The foot became infected with tetanus, and he died a few days later. He was twenty years old. My mother was sixteen, and two or three months pregnant with me. After my father died, they cut off my mother's hair, so she was bald like a nun or a monk, and they put the white veil on her head.

If you are a Hindu widow, you practice celibacy; there is no choice. A normal mother wears the colorful saris, the jewelry, and the red dot, the *bindi*, on her forehead, which represents the feminine goddess energy. The jewelry, the toe rings, the wedding necklace, and the black beads around her neck mean she is a married woman. But a widow is denied all that. During the funeral ritual, when my father's body was cremated, my mother had to give up the *bindi* and all her jewelry. After that, she wore only white and she looked really plain.

Centuries ago, a Hindu wife was expected to take her own life when her husband died; she was supposed to throw herself on her husband's funeral pyre. Now, she gives up only her jewelry. Either way, a widow has no life, even though she is still alive and even if she is only sixteen years old. After my father died, my mother left her husband's family and went back to her parents' house in Koru-Tadiparru, a village close to Guntur, where I was born. My earliest memories of my mother were of her being sad, really sad, because of losing my father at such a young age.

My family are Brahmins, the priestly caste in India, and my grandfather was an orthodox Brahmin priest. After my father died, my grandfather gave my mother a gift: he initiated her into the Vedic spiritual practices. Now that she was a widow, she could practice something higher, something more purposeful. So he taught her the saintly path, which is one way to worship the divine in Hindu religion. It is the way of detachment. Enmeshment with children and family are considered distractions to saintliness, so my grandfather trained my mother to be detached from life and from me.

My mother was always meditating, often for an entire day or week at a time. I couldn't get her attention, she was unapproachable, always engrossed in this blissful state. Sometimes I would cling and nag or cry, and that annoyed her. Other times she would let me sleep on her lap as she chanted, and it was very pleasant, like listening to a lullaby, half asleep. Often she was physically away, spending days and days in the temple, without food, without sleep, doing the *bhajans*, the ritual singing and chanting. She followed gurus, and when she traveled with them, she would leave me behind with my grandparents, which I resented. I had four uncles and an aunt who were close to me in age and, looking at how my grandmother was and the other mothers I knew were, I felt left out and neglected. But material life was too painful for my mother; and the spiritual life was a way of avoiding it—it gave her happiness, it satisfied her, so she stayed in it.

There was more ritual, more singing, more prayer in our house than in our neighbors' houses. My family was religious to start with, and when my father died it became even more religious, out of grief. I often saw people in my family going into transcendent states, ecstatic trances with emotional chanting and tears. We had a prayer room by the kitchen for the family deity, God Vishnu. My grandfather led the *puja* ritual there, saying the prayers and chanting the mantras.

In our household it took two hours to do the morning chants, mantras, prayers, and meditations. People got up at five or six o'clock every morning to do them. After that, my grandfather had his lunch and walked three miles to the village where he was the high school principal. When he came home in the evening, before and after supper, he and my grandmother and mother repeated the rituals. We children were awed by my grandfather. He was unapproachable too, a strong, silent person, except when he taught us our schoolwork, which was two or three times a day. His way of taking care of the children was teaching us and having us do homework assignments. There was no modern-age parenting there.

My village, Koru-Tadiparru, was hot and flat and dry. We had rice fields, and two lakes, one outside the village for drinking water and the other near the temple for washing the water buffalo, the cows and the bulls, the clothes and the dishes. Each caste had its own street, so all the families on our street were Brahmins. Everybody knew who they were and no one asked questions.

There was a lot of poverty in our village, including in my grandparents' home, even though my grandfather taught high school and owned some farmland outside the village. We weren't very fancy people, not so well-to-do. We had no cosmetics, no soap. We washed our hair with shampoo made from fruit, and we used some organic stuff, like corn flour, to wash our bodies. We grew most of our own food: vegetables, rice, and lentils.

The house itself was simple, a roof thatched with rice stalks and palm leaves, walls made of bricks and concrete, and a cement and tile floor. We had the prayer room, a kitchen, one big bedroom, and a hall where the children slept together on the floor and where my grandfather taught us our lessons. My grandparents slept in the bedroom, but later they slept in the hall and my oldest uncle and his wife had the bedroom.

The Brahmins are the highest caste in India, but not the wealthiest. They perform the rituals in the temple and in other peoples' houses, and many are teachers. My grandfather was a teacher, my oldest uncle is a teacher, and now I see myself as a teacher. But we weren't wealthy, the wealth we had was the spirit, and that's what stood in my heart.

In my village, the other castes had more money. The two merchant class families owned the two grocery stores. The labor castes were pretty wealthy because they owned land, worked in the fields, and did blue-collar jobs. The untouchables, the lowest class, didn't have land. They worked in the fields, cut hair, made shoes, jobs like that. If a water buffalo or cow died, they carried it off and made shoes out of the leather. A lot of poverty in that caste. Even now when I go to India, it brings up a lot of sadness in me.

Koru-Tadiparru had two temples, one for God Vishnu, the Preserver, and one for God Shiva, the God of Destruction and Re-creation. There are many gods and goddesses in Hinduism—Shiva, Vishnu, Goddess Lakshmi, Goddess Parvathi, and many more. Deep within the Hindu philosophy there is no form. Everything is divine, the universe is God, God consciousness, God manifesting. At the same time the divine takes the form of many deities; there are lots of personal gods, and you can worship them.

The two temples were made of big gray stones held together with cement. Even though they were only village temples, they were big—as big as our house here in Walnut Creek. Outside, there was a stone wall, the lake, and a garden with jasmine and hibiscus. My mother spent a lot of time in the temple, doing the rituals, dressing the deities, singing, reading scripture to the women, and helping the priests preach. Those are my memories.

We children used to gather cow dung for a special holiday in

January. We rolled the cow dung—it was heavy like mud—into a ball and drew mandala designs on it with rice flour, then we decorated it with flowers. We invoked the sacred energy into this menial thing and called it God Krishna. For me the sacred was nothing special, it was everywhere, in everything—in the cow dung as well as in the beautiful sky. There was no distinction between God and regular day-to-day life for me. Many people have a hard time seeing the God in the menial, in the downtrodden. But even now that's how I see the divine, in the lowly things.

I was fourteen years old when I finished high school, the first girl from my village to graduate. My engagement was settled by the time I graduated. The two families arranged the marriage. My husband is a cousin. That's a normal thing in India. My mother wanted me to have a college education, but she talked to my husband-to-be first, and between them the decision was made. I went to college. But I didn't finish. I passed the languages, but failed the science part, and so, when I was fifteen, she married me off. Now she could fully engross herself in her spirituality. But I was so young. Fifteen. I still needed parenting myself.

My husband worked in Calcutta as an electrical engineer, and we lived in a small apartment there. My first child, Lakshmi, was born when I was seventeen. Soon after that my husband went to the United States to work. I came later, when I was nineteen.

I couldn't believe what I saw, all these nice things. Big shopping malls, big clean streets, green lawns. But it was a lonely life. I was still basically a teenager, yet soon I had three small children of my own. My husband was working very hard as an engineer, so he was busy, and it was hard, living so far away from my mother. I couldn't travel to India to see her as often as I wanted to, and she didn't, and still doesn't, come here. She believes that if she crosses the Indian Ocean, she will no longer be a Brahmin woman, and her religious practices will be contaminated. I'm a woman with grown children now, but it's a trauma I still experience.

When my older daughter was about nine years old, she told me she wanted to take classical Indian dance lessons. Indian dance is very old. Hundreds of years ago, dance was part of the temple ritual. And now, here in the United States, the dance is returning to the temple. I found a teacher and pretty soon both my daughters and I were taking lessons and performing all over the United States.

For me, dance is moving meditation. Hindu tradition holds that God Shiva created the one hundred and eight postures of Indian classical dance when he danced the universe into being. Each posture forms a mandala, which is a design that emerges from the center and returns to the center, just as the universe continually emerges and returns to the center. In dance, the navel is the center, and the rest of the body forms the mandala. That center within the human body is God itself. That's why, when you do classical Indian dance, these intuitive flashes, these ecstatic occasions can happen to you. You connect with the spirit within.

The more I danced, the more spiritual I became. It was nothing of my doing. The practice itself took me there, just the doing of the dance. My dreams became more clear, and when I dreamed, I saw the deities, I heard the music. It became intense. I was shy, but the dance made me feel good. I gave talks and I opened a dance school here in my family room. I saw how classical dance could be used as therapy. Eventually, I earned a master's degree in counseling psychology and now I am a licensed family therapist. All of this because of my dance.

My spiritual practice now is partly sitting there, meditating. But it is also active, through dancing, teaching, and counseling. I see myself as a bridge between the sacred and the day-to-day. Unlike my family in India, I don't see religion, spirituality, and God as over there someplace, and the human being over here and not as valuable. My family in India saw raising children as duty and not as part of living a spiritual life. Praying, meditating, becoming one with God in the spirit, that was their reality.

I didn't have a mom who shared the family joys of children and grandchildren, but seeing her in that ecstatic, transcendent state was a blessing to me as a child. People who sat with her could feel it and, young as I was, so could I. My grandfather believed that the training he gave her was a gift to my mother, and now I understand that it was also a gift to me. As painful as it was for me, her detachment, her spirit, made me what I am today.

For my mother, spirituality still means being continually in that transcendent state. She strives for it even today. She goes on pilgrimages. She leads the life of an ascetic. She fasts day in and day out; she eats only once a day, and every two weeks she fasts one whole day. She is a guru herself now, and she is treated as a yogi—a monk or nun.

Several years ago, I was invited to dance at the Shiva-Vishnu Temple in Livermore. About one hundred people were there for the concert. I wore a red-and-white silk costume. My hair was in a long braid, which is a woman's most sensual ornamentation. A headdress and flowers crowned my head. I danced in the temple itself, before the shrine of God Vishnu, our family deity. God Vishnu was decorated with flower garlands. His eyes were closed, and one hand was extended in blessing. It was beautiful.

Each dance I did that day, I went into that ecstatic place. At the end of the program, I turned to the deity and bowed my face to the floor. I clasped my hands together and reached them out toward God Vishnu. It was a prostration, an offering to the universe, surrender. I offered myself to God. Whatever I needed to do in this life, I would do it as an instrument of God. Then I came back up and stood facing God Vishnu, still in that spiritual place, my consciousness still pointed toward the deity. My eyes were closed, and there were tears.

I opened my eyes so that I could see God Vishnu again, but there was the priest, standing in front of me, chanting the blessing at the end of the dance. He was holding the bowl of rice and flower petals to shower on my head and pour into my hands. The sight of him was distracting. Annoying even. A man was standing between me and the deity. My ecstasy dispelled, and the connection broke.

The priest took some of the rice and the flowers in his hand and reached toward me. I made a decision. It was an act of will, like co-creating with God. I bowed my head and cupped my hands to accept the blessing of the priest. I put aside my thoughts of the deity and acknowledged the spirit of God in the living being who was standing before me.

PART EIGHT: *Wrestling With Ego*

17

For Muslims—A 9/11 Wake-Up Call

One year, during Ramadan, I persuaded my editor at the *Contra Costa Times* to assign a story about how young, American-born Muslims practice Islam in America. As a result of that story I made contact with several young Muslims in our readership area. One of them, a woman, consented to be interviewed for this book. But later, without giving a reason, she asked that her story not be included. To protect the woman's privacy, I'll call her Yalda.

Yalda and I agreed to meet at an outdoor café in Berkeley. She was wearing *hijab*, so it wasn't hard to spot her: an ankle-length skirt, a loose-fitting shirt, and a white damask headscarf. She had pinned the scarf—she called it a *khimar*—under her chin then tucked its long corners in at the waist. The immaculate white of the damask framed a pretty face blessed with clear skin, a generous mouth, and no-nonsense eyebrows.

Born in the United States of Syrian immigrant parents, Yalda had lived in the same bucolic suburb for most of her life. She had attended the local public schools and was now an undergraduate at the University of California, Berkeley.

In my conversations with other Muslims I had learned that

obedience to God was at the core of her religion; a common translation of the word Islam is "submission to God's will." As we talked, I found out that, indeed, submission to God was central to Yalda's own faith. Like the runaway preacher Orenzia Bernstine, she thought of God as a loving, all-powerful, justice-dispensing God who knows what's best for her.

Unlike Orenzia, however, Yalda did not try to escape what she understood to be God's will. Even though she didn't fully understand why God would require women to cover their heads and most of their bodies in the presence of men who are not close relatives, she had begun wearing *hijab* a few years earlier, when she was seventeen. In doing so, she had obeyed what she and many other Muslim women believed to be a divine command.

Toward the end of the interview, as the two of us lingered at our outdoor table, Yalda, in her quiet, measured way, turned the conversation toward me. It went something like this:

"You are a Christian?"

"Yes. But I see the beauty in Islam."

That's how I respond whenever interviewees ask about my beliefs. A short answer, then change the subject. No use wasting valuable interview time talking about myself.

But Yalda was not so easily deflected. "Would you consider becoming a Muslim?"

"I was born into Christianity," I said. "It's the gift I've been given. It would be ungrateful to give it back."

The real reason I'd stick with Christianity, then and now, of course, was Jesus. My doubts and skepticism notwithstanding, I was deeply touched, and still am, by the idea of a God willing to take human form and to suffer pain, loss, and death alongside us. But a little interfaith tact was in order in conversing with this idealistic young woman. As a Muslim, Yalda would probably have to regard my thoughts about Jesus' divinity to be blasphemous, so I kept them to myself.

"But what if it was God's will?" Yalda continued. "What if God wanted you to become a Muslim. Would you submit to God's will?"

"Of course," I said without thinking. "Sure."

On the way home, I reconsidered that "sure." That was my Christian Sunday school upbringing talking. Like Yalda, I had grown up believing that religion was all about submission to the will of an all-powerful, all-knowing God—to an Other.

But now, thanks to Yalda's probing, I saw that it was time to reexamine that assumption. A little obedience to a higher power might be salutary for people with self-images bigger and fatter than mine. But for me, obedience, submission, to God was beginning to feel like a cop-out. Does God really hold all the wisdom and power, I wondered. Or is some of it—all of it—vested in me? Do I have agency? And if I do, isn't it my job to speak up when things aren't right in the world? Maybe God is depending on me to take some responsibility here. For that matter, what is God like, really? Is God an all-powerful Other . . . or something else? Is God out there somewhere and bigger and better than me? Am I less than God, and unworthy?

When I was fourteen years old, I clipped a poem, "Faith" by John Greenleaf Whittier (1867), from my church's Sunday morning bulletin. A few years ago I found it tucked away in the hymnal I was awarded as a member of the high school choir. The poem begins:

> *I bow my forehead to the dust,*
> *I veil my eyes for shame,*
> *And urge in trembling self-distrust,*
> *A prayer without a claim . . .*

That poem spoke to me as a fourteen-year-old. But it wasn't speaking to me now. Shame? Self-distrust? Trembling? My forehead in the dust?

Two of my interviewees, Ani Zonneveld, a Muslim, and Martin Verhoeven, a Buddhist, came to my rescue. They showed me where to look for God—within myself. They also helped me to understand an important distinction: subservience to an all-powerful, albeit kindly, judge who knows what's best for me is one thing. Spiritual surrender, relinquishing ego—while taking responsibility for one's moral choices—is quite another.

As the daughter of a noted Malaysian ambassador, Ani Zonneveld grew up all over the world. Her parents had set their sights on a career for her in the Malaysian diplomatic corps. But the young Ani was a musician at heart, and after college in the American Midwest she followed the siren song of the Western pop music scene to Los Angeles, where she quickly made a name for herself as a songwriter.

For our interviews, Ani invited me to her rambling house on the side of a hill not far from Universal Studios. On a wall in her dining room hung the Grammy certifications she'd won for her contributions to songs performed by blues singer Keb' Mo.' Waiting to find a place on another wall was a framed photograph and an invitation—to her as a leader in the progressive Muslim movement—for a Ramadan meal she and other guests shared with President Barack Obama at the White House.

Ani's story begins with a little girl trying to reproduce the ancient sounds of the Muslim call to prayer.

Ani Zonneveld—Her Story

Growing up I loved the sound of the Muslim call for prayer, the *azan*. When I was about twelve, being a musical kid, I started emulating it and reciting it on my own. But when my mom heard me, she freaked out. "No, no, no," she said. "You're not allowed to do the *azan*."

"Why not?"

"Because you're a girl."

And I'm like, "What? I can't recite the *azan* just because I'm a girl?" That was one notch against God.

Then when I started menstruating my mom told me, "You can't pray when you're menstruating, and you can't touch the Qur'an, because you're dirty." Yes, she actually used that word, "dirty." My mother was telling me again that God has a double standard—that I'm inferior because I'm a girl. All this generated a lot of negative feelings in me about my faith and about God.

But then right away I thought, what the hell? Is she serious? There's something wrong with this picture. It can't be true. I'm not buying it. Menstruation is natural. Right? Why would God create something and then deem it dirty? God created women to give birth. How can we be inferior to men? We're the ones who create this humanity. Why are we being punished? We don't want to bleed. It's a pain in the butt.

The larger Malaysian culture I grew up in was very open and accepting, however. Malaysia was, and still is, a multicultural, multiracial, multireligious society—a Muslim majority living alongside Hindus, Buddhists, Christians. There was a lot of spirituality in Malaysia when I was growing up, and most Malaysians were open-minded about religion. As a girl, I saw different people praying differently in Hindu and Buddhist temples that were just around the corner from each other. That's the environment I was raised in.

I'm in my early fifties now, and unfortunately the Islam of today—in Malaysia and around the world—is very different from how it was twenty-five years ago. My perspective of Islam is much more open-minded and loving in expression, more celebrative, than the conservative Islam we are seeing in so many Muslim countries. Even Malaysia has become very conservative. Sunnis are in the majority there, and because of the events in the Middle East, anti-Shia sentiments have become acute. Some people are even saying that you can't wish your Christian neighbor a merry Christmas or a Buddhist a happy Vesak. "It's *haram*, it's forbidden." That's the sad condition in Malaysia right now.

I was born in Malaysia of Malay parents, but most of my life was spent growing up overseas—Germany, Egypt, and India. My father—Abdul Khalid Awang Osman—was one of the youngest ambassadors appointed by the new government after independence from Britain in the 1950s. He was a go-getter, a very out-of-the-box kind of thinker, a doer. This carried over at home. If my father felt I was slacking off, he'd bring it back to education, to schooling, and to making your life count. He drilled that into me: "Make your life count."

When I was in Germany and about five years old, I attended a British school. Every morning we'd line up for assembly and say a prayer to Jesus. That's not what Muslims do, so I went to my mom and said, "We're praying to Jesus, what do I do?"

And my mom, though she was traditional about so many things, said something that still shapes the way I think about God, about religion and humanity. She said, "Oh, whenever there's a Jesus, just replace it with Allah and you're fine. We're all praying to the same God."

And so from then on, during prayers, whenever Jesus was mentioned, I would just say "Allah" quietly inside of me.

All the other children prayed with their palms together, but when Muslims pray, we cup our hands, as if putting them out for love or water. So during the prayer I'd put my palms together like the other children, then I'd crack them open just a little bit.

Music has always spoken to me. I studied classical piano for thirteen years as a girl, and on our travels from country to country I was always picking up the local instruments—tabla, sitar, guitar, organ, whatever I could get my hands on. When I was a teenager our family moved back to Malaysia, and I joined a local band, AsiaBeat, which was doing a fusion of jazz and traditional gamelan. We actually got a record deal with CBS, but my parents wouldn't have that.

"You're going to college," they said. "You're going do something useful with your life." And they packed me off to the United States, to Northern Illinois University in DeKalb, where I studied economics and political science. DeKalb was in the Midwest, in the middle of nowhere, but it had a strong political science department with an emphasis on Southeast Asia. The goal was for me to graduate, go back to Malaysia, and join the foreign service. It was all planned out for me.

Now, I have to tell you a story. It's 1981, I'm on my way to college in the Midwest for the first time, and I'm on a small plane sitting beside this elderly lady. Gray hair, very gentle, frail. And we have a really nice conversation.

The plane lands, and we are about to part ways when she asks me, "You seem like a nice young woman. What church do you go to?"

And I say, "Well, I'm a Muslim."

And she says, "Oh? I've never heard of that church."

I'm speechless. Wow! You mean there are people who don't know what a Muslim is? Where in heavens is my dad sending me?

But college in the United States was fantastic. I loved it. It liberated me and made me see the world differently. Being in America rewired my thinking. It taught me to ask questions. All this nonsense people crap on America isn't fair at all. Why do you think so many innovators come from America? It's the environment. You can do and be and think and say whatever you want here. You can ask questions, creative questions. That's my two cents as an immigrant.

As I said, since a young age music was my passion, no if's and but's about it. So I came to Los Angeles after college, hoping to find a way to make music into a way of living. I'd always had a knack for coming up with melodies and chord structures, so I bought some equipment and taught myself songwriting. That was a learning curve for me, a real slog. But I got enough writing work to support myself, and eventually I started collaborating with well-known songwriters. I had quite a lot of songs published and two of them won Grammy certifications, "One Friend" and "I'm Your Mother Too" sung by the artist Keb' Mo.'

I could do everything—lyrics, melody, production, arrangement, anything anybody wanted. I didn't write rap or traditional country, but I wrote everything else—pop, alternative rock, dance, kids' songs even. I can write a song in no time. I'm like a tailor. If you're the artist, and you want a song that fits your personality, I can sit down and get to know you, then craft a song that fits you.

But after a few years of this I began to feel I was just going through the motions, spiritually and emotionally void. I was writing songs because I was good at it. Even the Grammy certifications felt anti-climactic. I was pretty jaded. I thought, there's got to be something more important in life. A purpose. My dad, who had passed on recently, had always drilled it into me—make your life count. Contribute. Which he did himself in so many big ways; he's in the history books in Malaysia. And so, me being in Los Angeles, writing all these silly pop songs—it felt so mundane, so irrelevant. Big deal!

And then 9/11 happened. It blind-sided me. I thought, there's no way a Muslim could do this. Kill in the name of Islam—it's such an un-Islamic thing to do. Those bastards! And now still, every time I go through a security checkpoint at the airport, I cuss these guys out. The inconvenience, the mayhem they have created in the world in the name of religion because of their hate—whatever that hate is—is driving me nuts.

For me, 9/11 was personal. For a lot of Muslims it was personal. Personal because the idea of a Muslim driving planes into a building—acting with such an evil intention—was impossible. That a 9/11 could happen in the name of Islam was a shock to our psyche. But, unfortunately, many Muslims are in denial about the radicalism that has been happening in the Muslim world over the past twenty-five years. It's allowed an intolerant expression of Islam to take root—for hate to take root—and become the mainstream. For others—and it's taken time for us to accept this—9/11 is a result of a deep problem in Muslim society.

I was always conscious of God. I prayed, and I fasted during Ramadan, and I still do, but I can't say Islam was a big part of my life. Then 9/11 forced me to question my religion. It forced me into a box spiritually, and it forced me to dig myself out of that box. I did a lot of thinking during the months and years following 9/11, and I decided I needed to study the religion and relearn it. I made a promise to myself that I would surrender to that process: If I leave Islam because of it, then so be it. If I become closer to Islam because of it, then so be it.

I read the Qur'an, and I read books by progressive scholars of Islam, books on women's and gender issues, and books on the social context of the time the Qur'an was revealed. It was a slow process. But I discovered so much beauty in the Qur'an. This for example: "God will always be in wait, closer to you than your jugular vein." How beautiful is that?

I discovered an Islam that was much clearer and more loving than what I had been exposed to as a child and what was around me now as an adult. It liberated me from a lot of that cultural baggage: Not being allowed to do the call to prayer. Not being allowed to lead prayers in the mosque. Being told that menstruation made me unclean. I found out that these were all cultural accretions. They were not the Qur'an. They were irrelevant to Islam and, if anything, the revelations in the Qur'an counter the gender inequalities I was introduced to as a child. I got madder and madder: What is this nonsense? Why is this the norm? Why was I taught this in the first place?

My idea of Islam was changing, but so was my music. I found myself at a turning point in my work as a musician as well as in the practice of my faith. It occurred to me—I can write a song in my sleep, why not write an album of Islamic pop songs, in English, for an American audience? That grey-haired Midwestern woman I'd met on the airplane when I was eighteen years old—what would she think of Islam right now given the toxic environment we were in? That Muslims are all terrorists? I decided to do a song, an album, not just for American Muslims, but for that grey-haired lady and the rest of America.

My CD, "*Ummah* Wake Up," reflected my newfound Islamic values. I was very happy with it. So I was shocked to find out that, of the many Muslim retail stores in America, only two would carry it. The reason they gave was—and they would actually tell me this in my face—first of all, you use instrumentation: guitar, keyboard, and bass are *haram*, forbidden. According to them, Islamic music must only use the male voice and percussion instruments. And, secondly, you're a female singer. That's really *haram*. That's taboo.

And I'm thinking, holy cow! We're back to when I was twelve years old and forbidden from doing the *azan*. But now I'm experiencing this in America, in the land of the free. I was livid. I knew from relearning Islam that for centuries we have had Muslim women singers accompanied by musical instruments. And for someone to tell me in the twenty-first century that a woman's voice is *aurat*—too revealing, and therefore too sexually stimulating to a man, well, that was a distortion of the religion, a sexualization of the religion. How bloody annoying. I was not going to have it.

My CD turned out to be the first Islamic pop CD with full instrumentation that anyone, male or female, had done in English. No one was doing Islamic English pop, let alone a female. Male artists at the time were basically doing either rap or *nashid*—vocals and percussion only. I like to think that my CD helped free some people from those restrictions, because within a few years of my CD coming out, male Islamic artists were also writing spiritual songs in English with full musical arrangements.

Since then my Islamic music has evolved. My songs were upbeat at first, rah-rah, let's-do-this, pop stuff. But my most recent CD, *Islamic Hymns*, is more choral, more classical and spiritual, with lyrics from the Qur'an and famous Muslim poets like Rumi and Rabi'a Basri. When I perform these songs, sometimes there is this spiritual high for me. And I know that my music touches people. I've seen people tear up.

My music actually changes hearts and minds. When I sang the song "*Ummah* Wake Up" in front of a hostile audience not long after 9/11, I could see a change happening right in front of me—from cringing at the word 'jihad' to clapping and singing along by the end of the song. My dad's voice echoing to make my life count—I totally got it after that performance. All this time I had been doing music, it was a skill I was developing for a journey that was going to open up.

Meanwhile, it began to bother me that the community I was a part of—the mosque in Los Angeles—didn't fully reflect the real Islam I had found in the Qur'an and that I wanted to live by. People would say, "In this mosque we advocate for women's rights." And I'm like, "Oh, yeah? Then why do I have to pray in the back of the room? Why can't I give a sermon? Why can't I do the call for prayer? Are you kidding?"

Things started really bugging me. The gender issues and the cultural influences. Before Muslims pray, for example, we wash ourselves. But at this mosque and at mosques all over the world there's this teaching that if you touch someone of the opposite sex, the ritual cleanse you just went through is canceled and you have to do it over again—whether you intentionally shook hands with that person or just touched them by accident. Why? Because you were supposedly sexually aroused by this touching of someone.

This is not in the Qur'an, this sexualization of Islam. If you are shaking hands or hugging someone of the opposite sex who is a real brother to you in spirit, don't tell me that cancels your ritual cleanse. I'm so past that. It just doesn't jibe with Islam's concept of *ummah*—sisterhood and brotherhood and community.

That was just one of the many reasons I decided to start my own Muslim community. I had been part of a movement that formed soon after 9/11, the Progressive Muslim Union, but it fell apart pretty quickly. So I decided to start a group here in LA. I went to MeetUp.com and created a progressive Muslim meetup. People started signing up and within a month or two we had about twenty-five people. They were converts and Muslim-born people—teachers, business owners, tech people, retirees, full-time moms. We met in coffee shops and people's homes, once a month at first, then twice a month, then every week.

The first meeting was held in a coffee shop in Koreatown. For me, it was such a relief, a quiet hallelujah moment at finding so many Muslims like me. Even till now, when people discover us, the first thing they say is, "Oh, I'm so glad I'm not alone in thinking the way I do."

We found out that there were progressive groups in New York and Atlanta, and in 2007 Pamela Taylor and I organized a national founding meeting in New York, which led to registering Muslims for Progressive Values as a 501(c)(3) in the U.S. There are now several chapters in the United States as well as in Canada, Chile, France, South Africa, Australia, and Malaysia. To top it off it is now a non-governmental organization—an NGO—with a consultative status with the United Nations. It's catching on. It's making a difference.

The motto of Muslims for Progressive Values is—this is a community where you can be yourself and be Muslim. We are accepting of everyone—ex-Muslims who have come back to Islam, people who married outside the faith, gays and lesbians, people who felt they were pariahs because they thought differently from the rest of the pack. People in pain, because this is a faith they believe in, but couldn't find a loving space in a community—women who left their mosques because they were sick and tired of the misogyny; gay and lesbian Muslims on the brink of suicide.

Our community is inclusive of everyone, including sectarian differences. We're nondenominational—Sunni, Shia, Sufi, Ahmadiyya, or what have you. If it's a Shia leading prayer, we follow the Shia format. If it's a Sunni, we follow the Sunni. And we pray unsegregated, men and women together like we do in Mecca. We take turns, men and women, doing the *azan*, giving the sermon, and leading prayer. We are egalitarian.

Once, when we did our Eid prayer, a young woman said the verses in Arabic then English, Arabic then English. The addition of English is blasphemous for a lot of people. They look at Arabic as God's language. We're American Muslims and we're English speakers, and English is what resonates for us emotionally and your prayer should be in your mother tongue whatever country you're in. In Malaysia, it should be Arabic then Malay, Arabic then Malay. God can hear you no matter what language. It says that in the Qur'an, but human beings are so small-minded they think God is small-minded too.

Islam is actually an interfaith, inclusive religion. The word *muslim* with a small m means believer. That's all it was originally. But after Prophet Muhammad died, Muslim became capital m, which made it into an exclusive club. When a person says, "I'm a Muslim," with an exclusive capital M, that minimizes the bigness of God and the spiritual teachings of the Qur'an. I've become muslim with a small m—I don't have a problem embracing and praying in other traditions.

In our community I'm a reluctant imam with a small i, reluctant because I don't subscribe to a hierarchy. Islam is very democratic: the Qur'an states that we are all spiritually equal. An imam is simply someone who leads prayer. Anyone can do it. If you know how to lead prayer and the community says, "Hey, Barbara, can you lead prayer today?" you're an imam. I'm one of several imams in our community and because I'm certified to do the legal marriage papers for the State of California, I also officiate at weddings—many of them interfaith or same-sex marriages.

LGBT issues—this is another area where I think so many Muslims have gone off the track. There is no punishment in the Qur'an for being gay. But instead of following the Qur'an and the teaching of the Prophet Muhammad, many Muslims have followed contemporary homophobic interpretations against lesbians, gays, bisexuals, and transgender people. The extensive reading I've been doing of sound, scholarly, progressive Islamic theology backs me up on this. But also, on a basic human level, it seems to me that just as I was created to menstruate, gays are created the way they are. If I'm going to defend my right not to be discriminated against as a woman, then I have to apply that logic and sense of justice to other people's rights.

I think God is present everywhere. When the Qur'an says that God is closer to you than your jugular vein, to me that means God is in me, the spirit of God is in me. God has breathed life into our souls to make us living beings. Islam is similar to Native American practice in that sense: God is the creator, and an element of God is in everything created—in the universe, in atoms, in trees, in the soil, in the proteins of our bodies. God is in all of that. And God, the Creator, is creative, which gets expressed through our own creativity—in art, technology, business, whenever we think outside the box. That's all part of being godly, or godlike. Without creativity, we are soulless and disconnected from our Creator. But to be creative, we have to first be free to think for ourselves.

Muslims often use the phrase, "In the name of God, the Most Gracious, the Most Merciful." In Arabic it's "*b-ismi-llāhi r-raḥmāni r-raḥīmi.*" The root of that last word, *rahim*, is womb. To me that means the love and protection and nourishment of God is equivalent to that of a womb. And that is what's missing in so much of conservative and fundamentalist Islamic teaching today. The essence of the beauty and love of God is not taught. Instead, they teach fear, which is all about power and controlling what you think, say, and do. There is no room for individuality, no room for critical analysis or creativity. Asking questions is not permissible. It's not about you connecting with God directly. They want you to ask your sheikh. They want you to ask your imam. That is not Islam because we have been mandated to think for ourselves.

For me personally, God is not necessarily other. God is not an imaginable form that we as human beings with our human brain can understand. In the Qur'an's Arabic, God describes himself— itself, herself—as they, as we, as it, as he, and as she. God is a she. God is a he. God is an it. God is a we. God is all of that.

As for prayer—when we pray, who benefits? I mean really, God benefits? God doesn't need our prayers. Right? It's we who need that solace, that quiet moment to reflect. We are praying to God, but maybe we're just praying for our own sanity and our own peace—which we find in ourselves when we pray. Prayer makes us quiet down. Prayer forces us to reflect. And sometimes for me personally, if I'm going through difficult times, it breaks me down to tears. So much so . . . yeah, I'm tearing up already.

Sometimes I don't want to go there, because it's too painful, because it brings up these raw emotions. Sometimes it's very hard to process all those feelings. Sometimes it's better to keep yourself busy with life, and just go, go, go, so you don't have to slow down and reflect and to churn out these emotions.

At the core of Islam is submission to God, period. The word "Islam" is rooted in the Arabic word meaning peace. The two concepts—peace and submission to God—are connected. You are not just surrendering to God, you are surrendering to the God that is inside you, to yourself. You are surrendering to where that self takes you, to where that journey takes you, and what destiny holds for you. The Spirit guides you, and the Spirit is everywhere. You surrender to that Spirit and to that process. And in the process of surrendering you find peace.

When you don't surrender, when you think you control it all, you become even more stressed out. Some things are beyond your control. You can only do your best. Some doors just don't open. Other doors do, and when they do, you know this is what you're supposed to do. This is the path. But you have to be in a quiet moment to even see that. You have to connect with your own spiritual self to recognize it.

We're all created uniquely, and with that uniqueness comes a strength. Even if you have autism, you have a strength somewhere, and a gift. I think I am destined to be here in LA, destined to write Islamic songs and to be an imam with a small i in the progressive Muslim movement. I can hear my dad's voice, "Make your life count." And I think I have.

18

A Bowing Pilgrimage up the Pacific Coast

Unlike Savitri Hari, Martin Verhoeven rejected the religion of his parents. Born into a Catholic family, Martin spent eighteen years as a Buddhist monk and is now a Buddhist layman teaching comparative religion and Buddhist studies in Berkeley at the Institute for World Religions and the Graduate Theological Union.

When I first met Martin, he was living in a miniscule apartment with a gigantic view of the San Francisco Bay. The apartment was on the bottom floor of a house set on a steep Berkeley hillside. On the day of our meeting Martin—a small man with an elfin face and a well-tended beard—greeted me in the front yard and led me down some outdoor steps to his tiny apartment. Once inside I saw that, although he was no longer a monk, Martin still lived like one. He was able to shoehorn his life's belongings into two mini-rooms, with enough space left over in the kitchen to store his sister's upright piano. The dining table, which doubled as Martin's desk, faced the kitchen's sole window and its stupendous view.

Martin and I were sitting comfortably in the kitchen when, a couple of hours into our conversation, a fat black horsefly found its way into the apartment. It buzzed the kitchen window for a while, then gave it up and began throwing itself at my face. I felt an unholy urge to take a swipe at the thing. But I was a guest in a Buddhist's house. And in the Buddhist scheme of things, I reminded myself, even a horsefly qualifies as a sentient being, a potential buddha. I must treat this hairy, noisy nuisance with respect. Above all, I must not swat at it.

Noticing my discomfort, Martin stepped across the kitchen. "Let me show you something."

He slid the window open and put a large sheet of paper up against the pane of glass. Then he stood aside and held the paper so that sunlight shone through the open, unscreened window, but not through the glass. Sure enough, the horsefly made a beeline for the light and the open window, leaving me and Martin to resume our conversation in peace.

Our talk that afternoon ranged from Martin's Catholic boyhood and his rejection of Christian doctrine as a student at the University of Wisconsin, to the six-hundred-fifty-mile, two-and-a-half-year pilgrimage up the California coast that was his novitiate as Buddhist monk in the Mahayana tradition, to his decision to leave his Buddhist monastery just a few years before we met.

It's not uncommon for Buddhist monks to return to secular life after a time, Martin explained; his departure was not as radical a move as it might be for a Christian monk, say. When I pressed him for an explanation, I expected a practical rationale—a shift in career trajectory or frustration with the confines of monastic life. But Martin responded, characteristically, in strictly spiritual—and to me elusive—terms. "It wasn't that I decided to leave," he said. "I simply paid attention to the same deep urgings that had brought me into the monastery, and I followed them. In a sense, I haven't left the monastery at all. I steer by a passage in the Avatamsaka Sutra: 'One time is all time; one place is every place.'"

Martin's thoughts about the Catholicism of his childhood lent themselves more readily to words. He recalled learning the catechism as a small boy growing up in Appleton, Wisconsin. When asked, "Who made you?" he learned to say, "God made me." The next question, "Why did God make you?" was to be answered, "God made you to know and love and serve him in this world so that you would be happy with him forever in the next."

So far, so good.

Trouble came for young Martin when he was told that Adam and Eve, humanity's original parents, had sinned and as a result he, Martin, all of six or seven years old at the time, "had inherited the sins of somebody I didn't even know. It didn't make sense to me." Years later, Martin came to understand his youthful resistance to the idea of original sin, a doctrine that is central to many Christian theologies: "It's an unhealthy mind set. Instead of an innately positive view of human nature, you have this notion of something depraved and stained and deficient. Your only hope for a meaningful, fulfilled, happy, and wise life is to turn outside for relief, to accomplishments, possessions, or gods—in the Christian tradition, to Jesus Christ."

I'm not ready to follow Martin into Buddhism, but I like his thoughts on original sin: What kind of God would torment its creation with this enduring sense of flaw and inadequacy? Not the Christian God that I grew up with. When I was nine or ten years old, I came home from Sunday school one day with the news that, according to my Sunday school teacher, everyone in the class was a sinner and that sinners can go to hell.

"I don't like that word 'sinner,'" my mother said with an edge of bitterness in her voice that even my nine-year-old self could sense might have had to do with the years she spent as a girl in a Catholic convent boarding school.

Then she added, "There's no such place as hell."

And that was that.

For Martin, the sacred is to be found, not in an Other, not in the mighty God of the Abrahamic religions—Judaism, Christianity, and Islam—but in oneself, in equanimity in the face of death and life as it really is. It is found in releasing our grip on what we think are our possessions—jobs, things, relationships—and turning inward to listen to the urgings of the deepest self. It is quieting the ego. It is humbling oneself and becoming available to receive something new. "We are clay," he told me. "We shape ourselves by our thoughts, words, and deeds. If we work at it, we can become spiritual beings like Jesus and Muhammad and the Buddha. We can become *buddha*, which means awakened."

I don't expect to become anything like Jesus or the Buddha any time soon. But I do entertain a modest hope that I am becoming a little like Martin. It's all about ego, Martin keeps telling me. It's the need to be right that gets in our way. And in my case, at this moment, it's the need to wrestle God to the ground, demanding to know exactly who and where God is. Spiritual surrender—some think of it as obedience to the will of God, but from Martin I learned to think of it as an openness to God, to whatever God is, to the universe as it truly is.

Martin's story begins in 1976 outside a converted mattress factory in San Francisco's Mission District.

Martin Verhoeven—His Story

My girlfriend dropped me off at the monastery. It was an austere, simple-looking place in the San Francisco Mission District, a converted mattress factory with double glass doors and a sign, "Gold Mountain Buddhist Monastery."

"You sure you want to do this?" she said.

"It's only seven days. I can take anything for seven days."

I grabbed my sleeping bag and duffel from the back of the pick-up and headed toward the glass doors.

I was twenty-nine years old, and seemingly I had a lot going for me—a Ford Fellowship at Stanford, a solid future as a historian of American foreign policy, an apartment in Berkeley, a faded yellow International Harvester pickup truck I'd bought second-hand, a credit card, a camera, a guitar, and, of course, the girlfriend. Spending a week meditating with monks who shaved their heads and didn't talk was going a hundred-and-eighty degrees in the opposite direction of everyone and everything I knew.

I had grown up Catholic in Appleton, Wisconsin, during the fifties and sixties. I wasn't a Catholic anymore, but I wasn't a Buddhist yet either. Still, something had drawn me to this place. For one thing, I had been having this strange dream lately. An older man wearing a robe with one shoulder bared, points to a mountain and says, "You go climb this," and I wake up sweating.

Then, a few weeks earlier, I'd seen a poster at the studio where I was doing Tai Chi. It was for a seven-day Buddhist meditation retreat, and it had a verse:

A thousand eyes see all.
A thousand ears hear all.
A thousand hands help and support
Living beings everywhere.

When I read that verse, I started to cry. Later, on my way out of the studio, I read the verse again. Same thing. Tears came to my eyes. I went away, had a cup of tea, came back and read it for a third time. More tears. So I thought, okay, okay, I'll sign up for this Buddhist meditation retreat, whatever it is and whatever it brings.

The Mission District at the time was a jumble of industrial shops and low-income housing, noisy with buses and freeway traffic and smells of tortillas and hot dogs mixed with diesel exhaust. Inside the monastery was a different sub-universe. Everything was clean and radiant and adorned. Red banners. The light fragrance of incense. Wedge-shaped yellow cushions arranged in rows like waves ascending toward the altar. And at the altar, three large golden Buddhas sitting in calm awareness.

About a hundred and fifty monks, nuns, and lay people knelt on the yellow cushions facing the altar, chanting and bowing to the rhythmic binging and bonging of bells and drums. This was 1976, when Eastern religions were just beginning to get a toe hold in the U.S., and I was taken aback to see people my age, European Americans as well as Asian Americans, bowing down to statues. Weren't these the very graven images forbidden by the Bible? Yet I felt strangely at home.

I took my sleeping bag and duffle to the back of the room and found a seat on a bench against the wall. A half hour later, a monk wearing a red robe walked up the center aisle between the cushions. All I could see was his back. He seemed to be in his fifties with a substantial, solid body. At the altar, he bowed three times and turned to face us.

It was the robed man in my dream. He took a seat on a raised platform. Everybody bowed in his direction, foreheads to the floor. I didn't. I wasn't going to bow down to anything or anybody. This was idolatry. Hogwash.

The monk in the red robe began to speak in Chinese. Some younger monks translated. In the middle of the talk, the monk interrupted himself to tell a story:

"A Buddhist teacher was visited by a scholar who thought he knew more than the teacher.

"The teacher said, 'Let's have some tea before we begin.' Then he poured tea into the scholar's cup until it overflowed onto the floor.

"'You idiot,' said the scholar. 'The cup is over-full.'

"'Ah, yes,' said the teacher. 'It is full in the way you are already full of your own opinions and ideas. There's no room for anything more.'"

This was an old story, the monk said. But it still holds true. "Often people come to a teacher, and they think, 'Oh, I already know everything.' And if they see someone bowing, they think, 'I'll never do that. That's too demeaning.' Some people are so full of themselves; all they want is to be praised."

There were a hundred fifty people in the room, but I felt a hot spotlight bearing down on me. I felt the monk was talking directly to me. He hadn't met me but he knew me better than I knew myself. I had met my match.

After the lecture the monk sat in a chair, and people gathered around. I stood at the back of the crowd, out of sight. Part of me wanted to draw nearer and acknowledge what I had failed to acknowledge earlier, that he was special and what he had said had gone to my heart. But how? Not with a handshake, and certainly not with an arm around the shoulder. It had to be a bow. Everybody was facing the monk. I thought, I can risk a little bow. No one has to see it. One quick bow and I'm outta here. Bow and run.

I got down on the floor in a low crunch. I glanced left and right. Nobody was looking. I bowed my head to the floor, and this great joy came over me, this sense of a burden being cast off, of not having to pretend to be somebody I wasn't. And that's how I came through the door of Buddhism. It wasn't intellectual, it wasn't even psychological, it was a direct experience from this place in myself I hadn't known was there. It happened so quickly that I couldn't filter it with logic or reason or culture or previous beliefs. There was no time to say I should or I shouldn't. It was systemic and unmediated.

When I looked up, the old monk was peeking at me over the rows and rows of heads, a big, mischievous smile on his face. When people saw their Master craning to look my way, the crowd parted. Now, everybody was looking at me.

"How did that feel?" the monk said. "Did it hurt?"

A week or so later, my girlfriend pulled up in front of the monastery in my truck. I was ready to go back to my life with all its perks and pleasures. Part of me felt I should return home. But a stronger impulse wanted to stay. I had been eating vegetarian food, and without all the partying and drinking I felt pretty good. I hadn't hugged or kissed anybody in a week and, feeling strangely content, I was thinking, geez, maybe I'll try a little of that celibacy stuff, too.

And so, for the next four or five weeks, I went back and forth between the monastery and the apartment. I'd be at the monastery for the day, then I'd call the apartment and say, "Gosh, it's late. I'm staying overnight." It was the classic religious dilemma. I'd heard the story a hundred times of Jesus saying to the fishermen, "Drop it all and follow me."

Being a sensitive, bright woman, my girlfriend picked up on my ambivalence. The final straw came one evening. Things were getting romantic, and I said, "Now, you know that celibacy practice that the monks have—"

My girlfriend gets up, throws my guitar in the fireplace, goes to the bathroom and locks herself in. "There's nothing to live for!" she shouts through the door. "I'm going to take my life!"

I hear water running and a pill bottle opening. Oh, my God, I think, pacing back and forth. If I leave, she might take her life. What am I going to do?

I know, I'll call the Master and get some advice.

But it's eleven o'clock, and you don't just call and ask to talk to the Master at eleven o'clock at night.

I am desperate.

I call anyway.

A groggy monk picks up the phone. "Hello?"

I say, "This is Martin. Martin Verhoeven. I've got a problem here. I need to talk to the Master."

"Are you kidding?" the monk says. "The Master doesn't talk on the phone, especially at this hour!"

Click, another phone picks up. It's the Master. "*Zuma yang?*" he says. "What's up?"

"Oh, it's nothing," says the monk. "It's just—"

"Who?" says the Master. "What's happening?"

I blubber my troubles into the phone. While the monk translates, I'm thinking how terrible my situation is and how glad I am that my teacher is going to help me.

There's a long, calm silence on the line. Then, "So? Nobody's dying, are they? Who's dying?" Click. The Master hangs up.

And I go, "That's it?"

And the monk says, "That's it. Good night."

I put the phone down. I was stunned. The way the Master had spoken was like a pail of cold water thrown in my face. My girlfriend probably wouldn't really take her life. I knew that. *She* wasn't dying. But if I didn't make the right choice, maybe it was me who was dying.

I stood next to the phone, frozen. Five minutes passed. Silence in the bathroom. Finally, the bathroom door unlocked, and my girlfriend came out. We had a conversation, and finally she said in resignation, "Well . . . okay."

The next day I phoned my thesis advisor at Stanford to tell

him I couldn't in good conscience take the fellowship money any more. Then I packed up and went over to the monastery.

The Master was the Venerable Master Hsüan Hua, a Chinese monk who was born in Manchuria in 1918 and received the teachings of the Wei Yang lineage of Chan Buddhism from the Venerable Hsü Yun. Master Hua came to San Francisco in 1962, where he founded the Dharma Realm Buddhist Association and eventually dozens of temples and monasteries around the world.

What began for me as a stream quickly became a rapids. I was sitting at the evening ceremony one night when a monk from Toledo, Ohio, knelt before the Master, put his palms together, and vowed in front of everyone in the hall to make a traditional bowing pilgrimage from Los Angeles to Northern California: three steps and a bow, three more steps and another bow, and so on.

This monk was about my age and he had been at Gold Mountain Monastery only six or seven months longer than I had. He had been given the dharma name Heng Sure, which means "constantly real, genuine." I didn't know Heng Sure very well, but as I sat there at the evening ceremony, eyes closed, I had a vision of the two of us bowing together up the California coast.

The Master was saying, "Well, you can't do these things alone. This kind of pilgrimage requires an assistant."

Right away, I stood up and announced. "I'll do it. I'll go along."

There was this dead silence in the hall. Everybody was looking at me. I saw that one needed to do this kind of thing formally, so I went and knelt down alongside Heng Sure, put my palms together, and said I would go with him.

The Master closed his eyes. A long pause. Then he said in English, "Okay. So it is now time."

Heng Sure's vision was to take a vow of silence and make a pilgrimage up the California coast. It would be a repentance pilgrimage to turn back the world's conflicts, disasters, and calamities. He—and I—would be working on ourselves as we bowed along. We would be changing the world by changing ourselves.

I had more of an Audubon-John Muir type idea of what this would be like. The two of us would bow along the coast through cathedrals of redwoods communing with nature, Heng Sure in his monk's robes and I as Marty the layman in my jeans. He would be taking a vow of silence. I would be looking after him—setting up camp, hauling the gear. I'd wash his clothes and cook for him as he bowed along, kind of a "man Friday." In Chinese it's called a *hu fa*, or Dharma protector. Also, I had my black belt in Tai Kwon Do, and one of my ideas was if anybody bothered Heng Sure along the way, I'd take care of him Kung Fu style.

Immediately I started getting stuff ready. With my layman's money I bought cooking gear, new sleeping bags, and canvas-like jackets with hoods that were the de rigueur of cool in Berkeley at the time. When the Master saw all that expensive equipment, he said, "Can I suggest you take only things nobody else wants? You'll have a lot less trouble."

But we didn't listen.

Very quickly, in the midst of all this preparation, it dawned on me that I was not going to do this pilgrimage in jeans. I was going to be a monk. I saw that here in the monastery, I was in with the germ seed nature of my being. This was who I was. In a private ceremony, Master Hsüan Hua shaved my head, handed me my monk's robes, and gave me a dharma name, Heng Ch'au, which means "perpetually bowing" or "constant pilgrim." I was now in less than a few weeks a Buddhist novice in the Mahayana tradition.

Back in my room I tried on the new robes. They were made of coarse cotton and were way oversized. Heng Sure and I were scheduled to fly to Los Angeles the very next day to begin the pilgrimage, and I wanted to be an awesome-looking monk. So I stayed up till one or two in the morning sewing at this old sewing machine in the clothes room of the monastery. The next day I was completely discombobulated. My robes were still too big. I was tripping on them at the airport, and I was still sewing them up on the plane. As for my head, this was the first time it had been shaved and it looked like a peach.

The pilgrimage began on May 7, 1977, from the Gold Wheel Temple, which was then a temporary temple in an old house in South Pasadena. Master had flown down to Los Angeles to see us off, and on the morning of our departure he called us to his quarters. He had something to say. We knelt in the usual respectful position for receiving a teaching, one knee on the floor, palms together. Heng Sure translated.

The Master was playful but serious. "If anybody threatens you," he said, "you can use no violence."

What about my black belt training? I thought. Yo! Me! Dharma Protector!

"I don't want you to even have thoughts of violence or anger."

"But—"

"What? You are bowing to get rid of conflicts and disasters, and you can't get rid of the violence in your heart? Don't you know that conflicts and disasters come from angry, violent minds?"

I didn't know what to say.

"I'll tell you what," he said. "I will help you. I will give you a secret dharma to use."

Yes! I thought. I'm going to get the real Kung Fu from China. Like that seventies "Kung Fu" show on television.

"Here's my secret dharma," the Master said. "It's the four unlimited minds: Kindness. Compassion. Joy. Equanimity."

That was it? That's the secret dharma? Thanks a lot. How could this possibly protect us on the mean streets of LA?

The pilgrimage started a few minutes later inside the temple. The monks and nuns and lay disciples gathered around us with incense and recited the Great Compassion mantra.

na mwo he la da nwo dwo la ye ye

na mwo e li e

pe lu jye di shau bwo la ye

pu ti sa two pe ye . . .

We bowed to our teacher, then we bowed out the front door of the temple and into the streets of LA.

That was my novitiate training as a Buddhist monk, a six-hundred-fifty-mile bowing pilgrimage, Los Angeles to Northern California. It wasn't the quiet monastic life of getting up at four in the morning, meditating quietly, having a little tea and a nice bun, then sweeping the monastery walkways. It was right on the streets of America—city streets, country roads, sidewalks, freeways. A quarter mile a day, a mile at most. One step, two steps, three steps. A full, five-point prostration with knees, elbows, and forehead touching the ground, palms facing up. Recite a repentance verse, "Of all the bad karma I've created through my own greed and aversion and ignorance, with my body, my mouth and mind, I now completely repent and reform." Then get up. Three more steps. And down again for another bow.

At night Heng Sure and I slept in this old wreck of a station wagon. It was a 1956 Plymouth, so it was already an antique by 1977, one of those cars out of the space age era with big fins and lots of chrome. We found it in the garage behind the temple in Los Angeles, and someone got it running for us—barely. We took out the back seat so we could meditate there mornings and evenings and use it as a moving camp.

Every morning, I'd drive the Plymouth ahead a quarter mile or so, park it, and walk back. Then we'd bow out to the wagon for our one meal of the day at noon. When we got to the wagon, we'd drop the tailgate, pour some water from a bucket, and wash the grime off our hands and faces. While Heng Sure sat in meditation, I'd cook the lunch over a Coleman stove somebody had given us—rice, vegetables, whatever people had left for us along the way.

Afterward, Heng Sure would continue bowing, and I would clean up, move the wagon another quarter mile, park it, walk back to Heng Sure, and continue bowing with him. By the time we came to the wagon again, the sun was setting and it was time to study by an oil lamp, meditate, and retire for the night.

Heng Sure's vision was to bow from Los Angeles to a new monastery called the City of Ten Thousand Buddhas near Ukiah, a hundred and ten miles north of San Francisco. We expected the pilgrimage to take a year. It lasted two and a half. It took us two or three months just to get out of Los Angeles. There we were, on the sidewalks of LA: dog crap, broken glass, cigarette butts, bubble gum, little boys with pea shooters, East Los Angeles street gangs. Everywhere we went people broke into the wagon. By the time we got to the Pacific coast and Highway One, everything nice had been ripped off. Sleeping bags, packs, jackets. The only things we had left were the things nobody else wanted—just as the Master had suggested to us at the outset.

From LA our route took us up Highway One to Santa Monica and Santa Barbara, then along the coast to San Francisco and Ukiah. Our teacher checked on us once or twice a month. He'd have another monk drive him in this old, gray Chevy Impala. We never knew when we'd see him. The Chevy would pull up, and our teacher would get out. He'd sit against the fender in his golden and yellow robes, and we'd be on one knee in front of him in our gray robes, palms together, hoping for a teaching. He'd check to see if I was using my four unlimited minds, and not my anger and violence.

He might answer questions about the Avatamsaka Sutra, which was our reading for the pilgrimage. Heng Sure had his master's degree in Chinese from UC-Berkeley, and every night he'd teach me a little Chinese. Heng Sure communicated by writing notes most of the time, but the Master had said that Heng Sure could talk when he was teaching me Chinese. In return, I would teach him shaolin and tai chi.

"But no *lwo swo*," the Master said. No banter, no gossip. "No talking about how four frogs have eight eyes."

During the first months of our pilgrimage, there were moments of loneliness. Heng Sure and I had no radio, no newspapers, just a kerosene lamp that we lit, this ancient Chinese text that we studied every night, and the rhythm of the bowing. At the end of the day, we'd get in that station wagon along the coast and there was nothing, just that lamp, the wind, and the sounds of the ocean, and the deepest, quietest solitude you can imagine. The very next day, we'd be in a town and a whole school full of kids would rush up to us and try to figure us out. Newspaper people. Cops. Then, poof, everyone was gone, and it was dark, and it was just me and the lamp and the ocean and this other monk who doesn't talk.

There was a certain equanimity that came from being monastic in the world. We were out there on the highway like a couple of homeless people, yet we had this ancient discipline. The two things, the highway and the discipline, interacted like tectonic plates rubbing together. And all that rubbing over the months smoothed our edges in a slow and subtle way. The loneliness gave way to a fullness, a deep contentment.

People often asked us as we went along, "Who are you bowing to?" and I would say I wasn't bowing to anybody, I was humbling myself and opening myself up to receive something new—the way I had when I first met my teacher. I'd explain that I was bringing my mind to focused concentration, and from that concentration, insight would come, including insight into all the muck and garbage submerged in my own character, every mistake I'd ever made. Killing animals for food on the farm in Wisconsin. Chopping off a chicken's head. Catching a fish. Killing a bird with my BB gun. The things I had done to my body through drinking and partying. The hurting people sexually. The deceptions.

Buddhism teaches that change is possible. If you make a mistake, you just say, "I repent of it. I wish not to do it again," and go on. There is no need to wallow in remorse. We are clay, malleable. We shape ourselves by our thoughts, words, and deeds. If we work at it, we can become spiritual beings like Jesus and Muhammad and the Buddha. We can become *buddha*, which means awakened.

Every now and then evangelical fundamentalist Christians would come out and shake the Bible in front of us and try their damnedest to convert us. One day, when we were bowing along the coast near Cambria this big Cadillac stops, and a woman with these two poodles gets out and comes up to us, her high heels clicking. She asks what we are doing, and I explain.

"Well," she says, "I believe in Jesus, and Jesus gave me that Cadillac and Jesus gave me my two dogs, Fifi and Poo Poo, here. And Jesus gave me that nice condo on the hill. What did Buddha give you?"

By now we didn't have much. The Plymouth was rusting out from the coastal salt air, and I was having to push it to get it started. We were down to one robe each. And we had just enough rice for tomorrow's lunch.

"Look at you guys," the woman said. "You're in rags and dirty and everything."

All I could think of to say was, "Well, the Buddha gave me this Plymouth." But before I could open my mouth, she'd driven away.

A few days later our teacher drove up.

"Any questions?"

"Well, this woman said Jesus gave her this Cadillac and this condo on the hill. She wanted to know what the Buddha had given us. Teacher, what would you say?"

"I'd say that *buddha* gave me Jesus."

Like itinerant Buddhist monks everywhere, Heng Sure and I depended on donations from the people we met along the way. We had no money. People would hear about us and leave vegetables, nuts, or water on the hood of the Plymouth. Or necessities like tennis shoes, because they could see ours were wearing out. We'd go through a town and a mechanic would come out and fix the car for us and pour in some gas. Little kids would give us their peanut butter and jelly sandwiches on the way to school. A California Highway Patrol officer came up to us once and said, "My wife baked this cherry pie for you. Want you to have it."

That's how we went along. If people didn't see that we needed something, we just learned to get by without it. We didn't get too excited if people gave us food. And we didn't get too down if we went hungry for a day or two. And it was just as the Master had said. Once all our nice camping gear was gone and we were down to Salvation Army stock, no one bothered our stuff. We didn't even lock the car.

Somebody gave us a book on wild edible plants and I learned to forage. If we had some rice, I could find greens and vegetables to make a pot of herbs. I thought I was turning into a pretty good *hu fa.* One day I was especially pleased with myself. I'd read about fennel, which makes a wonderful digestive tea, and I'd discovered some growing along the road near Hearst Castle.

I was out there clipping fennel, and this car pulls up. A guy gets out. Khaki pants, mild-mannered, a Wally Cox, science teacher type of guy.

"Excuse me," he says. "What are you doing?"

I say, "Well, I'm a Buddhist monk. I'm preparing lunch here, and I'm cutting some fennel for tea."

And he says, "Well, I'm a plant botanist from Cal Poly. That's hemlock you're cutting, and what you have in your hand is enough to drop a cow."

"My book says it's fennel."

"It's hemlock, the same stuff Socrates took."

That wasn't the only mistake I made on that trip. At one point, Heng Sure and I were in Big Sur. We had been bowing for a year and a half, and we were still hundreds of miles from our destination. It was November or December, the rainy season in California, and the days were short and cold. We had wet clothes during the day and wet sleeping bags at night. We were miserable.

We were camped under the redwoods in a big state camping ground, reading the Avatamsaka Sutra in the back of the station wagon by the light of the oil lamp. The passage that night was about giving. It's called *dana*. "A bodhisattva is not stingy," the text said. "A truly wise person gives away what he has to benefit living beings."

Well, just as we finish reading all about *dana*, this man comes along, and he's half naked, wild hair, scraggly, unkempt, unshaven, and smelly.

"Uh. You guys got anything?" he says.

At first we thought he was just a mooch. But then we started writing notes back and forth and we said, whoa, maybe this is a bodhisattva, a spiritual being, come to test us. Maybe it's a sign that we are spiritually blessed. We'll give him some of our clothes. So we gave the beggar a pair of monk's pants, a jacket, a wool hat, and a new pair of shoes.

"You got anything else?" the beggar says. "It's cold out here."

Now we're both thinking, oh, yes, this is a test from heaven, so we say, "Here, take our sleeping bags. Take our rubber boots. Do you need more food?"

Pretty soon we've emptied out the station wagon to this guy. Night is coming on. The wagon has no heater. And the beggar is gone.

Heng Sure writes on his notepad. "We forgot to bow to him."

I nod. I was thinking the same thing. We'd missed our chance. If we had bowed to the man, maybe he would have given us enlightenment.

Pretty soon a park police car pulls up with its lights flashing, and he's got the beggar by the scruff of the neck. "Excuse me, venerables. This guy claims you gave him all this stuff. Is that true?"

We nod our heads. "Uh-huh."

The ranger is this square-jawed, square-shouldered, Midwestern sort of guy. He looks at us like we didn't understand what he just said. "You know, we've been having a lot of thievery in the campground, and we're pretty sure this is the guy . . ."

And he's looking in the back of our station wagon, and there's nothing in it.

". . . I mean, he didn't hold a knife on you or anything?"

"No, no, officer."

And we're putting our palms together, thinking now's our chance to bow to the beggar. We each do a little head bow. And the cop says, "Ooooo-kay," and takes the guy away.

A few days later the old gray Chevy pulls up, and we're on one knee telling our teacher all about the beggar and the park ranger.

Our teacher shakes his head. "So stupid. You guys have no wisdom whatsoever. Buddhism is about not seeking anything. You stopped seeking pretty women and nice cars and you became monks. And now you are seeking spiritual attainments. Same greedy mind, different object."

"Oh. This wasn't a bodhisattva?"

"No," our teacher said. "Probably the real bodhisattva was the park ranger giving you a chance to get your stuff back."

We felt so naïve, so humiliated. It was the park ranger, not the beggar, who had given us the teaching. He had shown us things as they really were, which is the Dharma. But we had our own reality: "We're ready for enlightenment here. We've spent a year and a half on the road. We're cold. We're tired. Give us the fruit—now."

Our teacher shook his head. "Anything you seek will obstruct you, and that includes spiritual attainments and miraculous signs." Then he opened the trunk of the Chevy and gave us all his clothes.

Heng Sure and I could see our faults and bad habits very clearly out there on the highway, and so could the people we encountered along the way. There was no place to hide. We were transparent. The ancient monastic discipline that our Master had insisted on was our only protection. But it was a powerful protection, and I credit it for saving my life at least once.

Heng Sure and I were bowing through a fairly remote area of the Big Sur coast when I noticed this guy following us in a beat-up Jeep. The CHP had been warning us about this stretch of highway. They had found body parts in the hills around here. And somebody had been blown away in a bathroom at one of the beaches.

That morning I had parked the station wagon on a pull-out

at the edge of a cliff overhanging the ocean. When we got to the wagon at noon, nobody else was around. We ate lunch and Heng Sure began his bowing. He was out of sight and I was cleaning up the dishes, when this Jeep pulls up and parks between me and the road.

A stocky, rough-hewn kind of guy is in the driver's seat. He doesn't say a word. He looks around, then reaches under his coat and pulls out a revolver. It's a forty-five probably. He cocks it and aims it at me.

I'm standing at the edge of a cliff. There is no place to run. My instructions are not to fight. I'm not to use my anger or react with violence. That leaves me one choice. I face the man. I put my palms together. I drop to one knee and lower myself into a deep bow.

After a moment, I come back up. The man is still there. The gun is still there. The man is looking at me intently. I feel fear, but it isn't an overwhelming fear, because I know that this pilgrimage is exactly where I'm supposed to be right now, and whatever will happen will happen.

The man slowly releases the cocked trigger. But he keeps the gun pointed at me for a while. Then he puts the gun back under his coat, nods, and drives away. That's the last I see of him.

People talk about the power of prayer, but I was seeing first-hand that it's not the power of the prayer, it's the power of the mind that is willing to be totally sincere, totally upfront, totally letting go, and totally emptied out. Kindness, compassion, joy, and equanimity, the Master's four unlimited minds, aren't platitudes. They actually work.

After that, Heng Sure and I continued bowing and walking for nearly a year. On up Highway One, through San Francisco, over the Golden Gate Bridge, up Mount Tamalpais, and back to

Highway One. The Pacific Ocean had been a constant presence for most of our journey, and now, on a sunny day in October 1979, with a wonderful breeze blowing off the ocean, we were approaching the Boonville Road, a lightly traveled two-lane highway barely visible on California road maps, that would take us east, away from the ocean, and over the coast range mountains toward the Ukiah Valley and the City of Ten Thousand Buddhas.

We had a last, solitary, calm moment on the seacoast, then we changed direction and faced east. As we began our ascent up the Boonville Road, I felt a shift and a turn. In the midst of a bow, I saw myself and all the people I knew grasping for things, like basketball players going up for the ball. And I could see that it was all a self-generated spook. We were vying and competing, not because there was something valuable out there to be had, but because we didn't feel whole. It was one of those freeing insights I've been talking about, and it came with the breeze. It was a moment of equanimity. Not a high or a rush, but a happiness that was beyond getting or losing.

A few weeks later, we came within sight of the City of Ten Thousand Buddhas. A new great gate to the city was being built, and we were going to be the first to pass under it. Fog was settling among the towering valley oak trees that day. As we drew nearer, we could see the sparks from the welder's torch through the flat, gray mist, and then our Master's bright yellow-orange robes under the gate.

We approached our Master and bowed before him, a deep prostration. He rubbed the crowns of our heads in blessing, then we bowed on into the city. An assembly of close to two hundred monks, nuns, and lay disciples lined our path, chanting the Great Compassion mantra as we went—just as when we first began in Pasadena. The same mantra and circle.

na mwo he la da nwo dwo la ye ye
na mwo e li e
pe lu jye di shau bwo la ye
pu ti sa two pe ye . . .

We had expected our pilgrimage to take a year. It had taken two and a half. We had covered six hundred fifty miles of highways, roads, and sidewalks. But to our Master it was like, "If you think you have done a good job, if you want praise and recognition for what you have done, then you have missed the point. You have wasted two and a half years." We had arrived at the end of our pilgrimage, and yet there was no arriving. Our journey was just a beginning, and now we were back to the same foolish mistakes, the same lessons, the same tectonic plates rubbing up against the ego.

Heng Sure and I continued to bow out on the grounds of the new temple for three, four, five months after we finished the pilgrimage. I found it difficult to be indoors. Buildings, the heat, the confinement were uncomfortable. People chattering in an enclosed room irritated me. I was thinking, I'm going to go on and on like this, outdoors in the elements with the birds and the weather, away from people.

But that was not to be. Master Hsüan Hua saw that Heng Sure and I had become attached to our solitary spiritual practices, and he pulled the rug out from under us again. He sent us back to Los Angeles. There in the heart of the city, we started a new temple—with all the traffic and the noise and all these city people, Los Angeles types, coming and going all day long with their kids.

I used to go up on the roof at night to try to see the stars through the smog. Instead of stars, I'd see the helicopters with their searchlights. I'd hear the gunshots, the squealing tires, and the sirens. And I'd remind myself that one time is all time; one place is every place. My pilgrimage was not about the road. It was a pilgrimage of the mind, and this was what it had always been, and would remain. Upon our departure for LA, the Master had repeated the very words of instruction he had given us when we started out on the pilgrimage: "When you are out on the highway, be as if you never left the monastery. And when you are in the monastery, be as if you never left the road."

PART NINE: *Pinning God Down*

19

The One Thing I Know for Sure

I conducted the first recorded interview for this book with Anthony Mack way back in 1997, and here I am finishing up its last chapters a decade and a half later. Why did the writing of this book take so much time—this clumsy, painfully sincere, and probably naïve attempt to get a handle on the meaning of it all, to wrestle God to the ground if only for a nanosecond?

I can point to the usual distractions: blog, Facebook, Twitter, email. Children graduating from high school, going off to college, looking for jobs, getting married. A patient husband insisting on taking some nice trips abroad once in a while. A kitchen to remodel. A sewer back-up in the basement to attend to. An elderly mother whose closets I cleaned out, whose Christmas cards I addressed, and whose head I stroked as she took her last breath.

These things pulled me away from my writing, yes. But the real reason this project has taken so darned long is this: I was waiting for God—the Tao, the Ultimate Reality, the I Am That I Am, or however it is that God wishes to be addressed—to show up in my life and write the ending for me. A nice dramatic, marketable ending, please, one that will make sense of the many disparate voices I've been recording all these years.

Didn't happen.

Some people—Robert Tharratt, Orenzia Bernstine, and Stace Hall—are blessed with tidy, tellable stories with dramatic turning points. Not me. I'm just a regular, garden variety person, a hopeful, church-going skeptic whose moods jostle between doubting, seeking, hoping, believing—and right back to doubting. Like Martin Verhoeven, I've been on a journey where there is no arriving. That's me. And it's taken me all this time—and the wisdom of the dozens of people I interviewed for this book—to realize that I had my answer all along.

A meeting with a Hindu guru I met while on the religion beat for the *Contra Costa Times* comes to mind. She was Mata Amritanandamayi, and she had an ashram near Castro Valley in our circulation area. Our interview was too brief to shape into a first-person narrative—the whole conversation fit onto a single page of a reporter's notebook—but that encounter is a good example of how we learn something once and then, looking back on it several years later, we learn the lesson all over again in a new way.

The story begins on a light-filled summer day.

Mata Amritanandamayi—Interviewing God

The grassy hilltops were bright with summer sun as cars, station wagons, and pick-up trucks bounced down a narrow gravel access road into the deep canyon below. I followed the caravan downhill in my old yellow Volvo station wagon, a reporter's notebook tucked into my purse along with a fistful of pens. We were heading for the Mata Amritanandamayi Center, a sixty-five-acre Hindu ashram in the undeveloped hills adjoining Castro Valley, and I was on assignment for my newspaper.

Down below, men wearing loose-fitting white trousers and shirts waved the drivers toward parking spots in the grass. One of the men directed me to a place in the sun. I left the station wagon and joined the men, women, and children—there were hundreds of them that day—as they made the last dusty quarter mile to the ashram on foot. Some had come here from nearby cities and suburbs. Others had begun their pilgrimages as far away as Pennsylvania, India, and Germany. Later in the day, the pilgrims would make the final lap of their journey, and they would make it on their knees.

Ammachi was here. Ammachi—Mata Amritanandamayi—had come all the way from India to visit her San Francisco Bay Area ashram. And while she was here, she would receive, bless, and embrace—literally—each one of the hundreds of devotees who came to see her. My editor and I had talked about this story for months, and now I was finally going to write it. It would be a good story, I thought, a big one.

Until today, the Mata Amritanandamayi Center had kept a low profile, tucked away as it was in the hills. The ashram had been founded some years earlier, time enough to build a splendid prayer hall with high beamed ceilings, skylights, balconies, and a gift shop, but not enough time for its leaders to become completely comfortable with publicity. The ashram's adjoining neighbors had had reservations about the sudden dusty rush of automobile traffic. And it wasn't clear what the center's more distant neighbors, some of them conservative Christians, would think of this place—a singing, chanting, meditating, vegetarian community founded by a Hindu woman whose embrace, it was said, conveyed the divine.

I'd done some reading in preparation for today. I'd also interviewed the swami in charge of the center, and I'd telephoned all over the country to hear what other Hindu organizations had to say about Mata Amritanandamayi. An official at the Hindu Temple Society of North America had told me that Mata Amritanandamayi—also known as Amma, or Mother, and Ammachi, Holy Mother—was held in high esteem in India and that her practice of hugging her devotees, each one of them, distinguished her sharply from other gurus. He couldn't vouch for the people around Ammachi, but as for Amma, "She's definitely connected to God. There is no doubt about that."

And so, I was prepared. I had done my research and now, today, I was here for the real thing—a *darshan*, an experience, of Ammachi herself.

Mata Amritanandamayi was born in 1953 in a fishing village in South India's Kerala province. She left school early, after the fourth grade, to stay home and help her family. She was a pious child whose ecstatic experiences bewildered her family and village. At age twenty-one, the story goes, she attained enlightenment and became one with the Divine Mother. Those who knew her began to see her as a manifestation of God's maternal love for humanity, and soon devotees from India and the West began arriving at her family's doorstep.

In time, Ammachi's followers numbered in the millions, her disciples report. With the financial help of her numerous ashrams around the world, she established schools, temples, a hospice, and a medical center in India. In 1990, she sent Swami Paramatmananda, a European American originally from Chicago, to lead the Castro Valley ashram.

Ammachi's devotees stopped at the entrance to the prayer hall to take off their shoes. I removed my own shoes, left them outside, and followed the others indoors. Inside the hall, the sound of sitar and drum mingled with human voices. Hundreds of devotees, chanting, clapping, and meditating, sat on the floor facing a platform at the far end of the room.

A small, round form in gauzy white—a woman who looked to

be in her forties—sat at the platform's edge. Her hair was wispy and black and was tied at the nape of her neck. Her face was wide, and pretty. A red dot encircled with white marked her forehead. She was smiling broadly, as if someone had just given her some good news.

Ammachi's devotees sat in neat lines on the floor. It would be hours before many of them reached the front of the room to present themselves at Ammachi's feet and receive her embrace. Meanwhile, they would wait, meditating, singing, and feasting their eyes on their guru.

I slipped past the gift shop to the front of the hall to get a closer look. There, devotees were rising to their knees and moving toward the small woman in white. Ammachi put her arms around each one and pressed their bodies close to hers. They rested their heads on her shoulder; she kissed them and spoke into their ears. Then, with a luminous smile, she gazed into the eyes of each one and pressed a small gift, a flower petal or a chocolate, into each palm. There was no rushing Ammachi. She took her time, and many left her side in tears. Some lingered on the platform behind her, sitting or kneeling to face her. Many of them bowed forward and touched their foreheads and hands to the floor.

I pulled out my reporter's notebook and took notes. What would it be like to be held in this woman's embrace, I wondered. Was she a mystic? A sage? A saint? A mahatma—a great soul? Could she be, as some claimed, an avatar—like Jesus, an earthly embodiment of God? Could her embrace convey the divine?

I wandered over to the gift shop. Ammachi dolls, Ammachi song books, and Ammachi tote bags were offered for sale alongside statuettes and painted likenesses of the usual Hindu deities. I bought a book recounting Ammachi's life story and tucked it into my purse.

Outdoors, a number of devotees were preparing a large, sumptuous vegetarian meal set out on long tables under awnings: rice, lentils, soul-satisfying curries. One of Ammachi's devotees had been appointed to answer my questions today. I asked around for her and found her under an awning, helping with the food. She was a friendly European American woman in her thirties or forties.

"Would you like to meet Ammachi?" she asked.

Without thinking I said, "Yes."

I paused to reconsider. What would meeting Ammachi require of me? Would I have to kneel? Would I have to let myself be hugged?

As a newspaper reporter, I liked to keep a low profile while covering a religious event. I'd go through just enough of the motions to be unobtrusive, but I didn't participate in the worship. It didn't feel right to make myself out to be an observant Jew one week, a practicing Buddhist the next, and a believing Greek Orthodox Christian the week after that. Given the slender faith that was mine, worshipping in an authentic way in my own Episcopal church was challenge enough. Besides, kneeling before another human being went against my Christian upbringing. For Jews, Christians, and Muslims, the God of Abraham is the one true God. Kneeling at the feet of this small round woman from Kerala would be apostasy—or so I had been taught.

"That's wonderful," my hostess said. "I'll arrange for you to meet her."

"Actually," I said. "I'd like to interview her. Rather than, you know, be hugged. Is that possible?"

With those words, my discomfort increased. I had just exchanged one predicament for another. What if this Mata Amritanandamayi really was a great soul? An emissary from God?

What if she was God herself? And if she was, how in the world do I interview her? How does one interview God? What questions could I possibly ask that would not be preposterous?

Maybe I should just get the hug and let it go at that. But I sensed my editor's kindly, professional face looking over my shoulder, reminding me that I was a newspaper reporter on assignment, and this was a community event. A congregation was welcoming its founder to town with singing, chanting, and first-rate Indian food. And I was going to interview her.

"No problem," said my guide. "An interview. I can arrange it. Meet me here in ten minutes."

I took some time to inspect the gorgeous food spread out on the long tables. The meal had been prepared by devotees doing *seva*, or selfless service. Much of the work of the ashram gets done by portioning out chores to visiting devotees, I learned. It was good for the soul, and good for the ashram budget.

But then my thoughts returned to the interview ahead. I took out my notebook and thumbed through it to a clean sheet. What do I say to this Ammachi? What do I ask? Most of my readers were Christian or Jewish; I knew what they would want me to ask—isn't it a blasphemy against God to present oneself as divine? Isn't it sacrilegious to allow others to kneel down in front of you? And how about those other aspects of Hinduism that snag the Western mind—can there really be more than one deity? Can some of them be female? Those were the questions my readers would want answered. They were questions I wanted answered.

My guide returned and led me into the prayer hall. We tiptoed through the crowd of seated and kneeling devotees. The closer we got to Ammachi, the harder it was to find a place for the next footstep. Sitting next to Ammachi, on her left, was a swami, an Indian probably, wearing a saffron robe. His eyes were dark and vivid, his nose beaked, and he had black shiny hair. He nodded toward me in greeting and made a place for me to sit on the floor to Ammachi's right.

The swami spoke with Ammachi in Malayalam, her native language. When he had finished, she turned to me and rained her luscious smile on me. What a lovely woman, I thought. So ordinary. The kind of person I'd chat with in the supermarket checkout line. Ammachi turned away from me to welcome the next devotee in line. She took the man in her arms, rocked him, kissed the top of his head and crooned in his ear.

"Do you have questions?" the swami said. "Ask them please. You have a few minutes."

A few minutes. Not enough time to warm up the interviewee with small talk. I'd have to be blunt.

"Yes," I said. "I have questions. I hope they won't seem too abrupt and disrespectful."

The swami nodded, encouraging me.

"Ammachi," I said, looking up at her now. "Many people would say that it is blasphemy to bow down to another human being and worship them as if they were God. What would you say to them?"

The swami translated.

Ammachi listened, then took the time to greet yet another pilgrim. When the devotee had moved away, she turned toward me and smiled as if to reassure me that my question was indeed excellent, going straight to the point.

"When you worship a mahatma, a great soul," she said, "you are not really worshipping the person. You are worshipping the divine quality in him."

I nodded.

"Great souls have a form like an ordinary human being," she said. "But at the same time, they are beyond that name and form."

I nodded again. I understood, but wondered to myself, did that mean Ammachi was a great soul? I studied her. There she sat. Round and pretty and dark and every bit the friendly supermarket shopper smiling back at me over a grocery cart.

I looked out over the prayer hall. Hundreds of faces were turned our way, each one of them waiting for a moment with their guru. I thought I had time for one more question, a small one.

"Ammachi, can God be female as well as male?"

"Yes," she said. "God is everything. If God is everything, he is both Mother and Father, Universal Mother and Universal Father."

With that, Ammachi and the swami turned their attention to the next devotee in line.

"Thank you, Amma," I said, nodding my head toward her knees. It was a nod, not quite a bow, signifying that if I were the bowing sort, I would be bowing right now.

Without standing up—that would attract too much attention—and without turning my back on Ammachi, I crawled, slid, and knee-walked my way out of her presence, my pen in one hand, my notebook in the other. I had my story. Outdoors, at a table, a paper plate heaped with rice and curry was set before me. I opened my notebook and made the last of my notes.

On another day, I had a chance to put some of my questions to Karen Kasturi Mattern, one of the dozens of devotees who kept the Mata Amritanandamayi Center running. Karen invited me to the bungalow in Berkeley she shared with her husband, who worked in the building trades. As we talked, the morning sun gleamed on the lace curtains and hardwood floors of Karen's living room. Yes, Ammachi was the real thing, she told me. "She's an incarnation of the Divine Mind of God, the Holy Spirit, just as Christ was. She's a stream of living water."

Karen, born in 1950, had grown up Catholic in Philadelphia. She had earned a Master of Theological Studies degree at the nearby Franciscan School of Theology and had taught religion. She encountered Amma for the first time a few years earlier, when a friend persuaded her to attend a *darshan* being held in a nearby church.

Karen sat and watched as Ammachi took the time to welcome and embrace each individual in the crowd. Later she concluded that "this must be what it was like when Christ lived. People came to him with a lot of need, and these people were doing the same thing—you could see it on their faces." Amma was sitting there as ordinary as can be, but her devotees were moved "down to the soles of their feet." Eventually Karen became active at the Mata Amritanandamayi Center, helping to run the ashram's soup kitchen in Oakland and adopting the name Kasturi.

Did she consider herself a Hindu now, I asked, or a Christian?

Karen smiled. She had heard this question before. "When people ask me that, I say I'm a little of both."

"How do you manage to be both?"

Her answer echoes the thoughts of Salma Arastu, Huston Smith, and Seyyed Hossein Nasr. "There is only one God," she said. "There are different symbolic languages for talking about him or her, different rituals that we participate in, and different communities, but the divine permeates the entire universe."

A few days after I turned my Ammachi story over to my editor, I drove the twenty-five miles out to Castro Valley to make my way down the dusty gravel road a second time. I was off duty today. I was on my own time. If a reporter's notebook was tucked inside my purse, it was because I rarely go anywhere without a notebook and pen. This time, I was making the trip because I still had questions. They weren't a reporter's questions. They were my own questions, and they couldn't be asked with words.

The sun was setting, and the prayer hall had already filled to overflowing. Ammachi sat at the edge of the platform, greeting devotee after devotee. I found a place on the floor and sat cross-legged, taking it all in. Who was this woman? I knew that for many of those sitting around me this evening, Mata Amritanandamayi was much more than the middle-aged daughter of a poor South Indian family; she was the sacred breaking its silence, the invisible making itself visible.

But who was she for me? A lovely human being, no more and no less, I was pretty sure. Still, it felt right to sit here, letting the sounds of the sitar, the drums, the chanting, and the hand-clapping wash around me. Finally it was my turn to approach Ammachi. I didn't expect her to recognize me from our interview, and I don't think she did. She opened her arms. I moved toward her on my knees and rested my head on her shoulder. It was soft, she smelled sweet and fresh. She wrapped her arms around me. Her body swayed, and she chanted something into my ear; it felt like a blessing—one that I needed, perhaps, but didn't know that I needed. Then Ammachi let go of me and reached into the basket beside her for a chocolate wrapped in foil. She pressed it into my palm. I thanked her and moved away.

The encounter was over, but I wasn't ready to leave this place just yet; something was keeping me there, some unfinished business. Walking on my knees, I squeezed my way onto the platform behind Ammachi. It was crowded with devotees, sitting, kneeling, facing their guru. Two teenaged girls, very pretty in bare feet and loose muslin skirts and blouses, knelt between me and Amma. I watched them as they placed their hands on the carpet, bowed, and touched their foreheads to the floor.

Those girls were on to something, I thought. I could do that. I could prostrate myself like that. But what would it mean if I did? Would it turn me into a Hindu? Would I have to give up Jesus? Would I have to eat vegetarian? I didn't think so. I decided to give it a try. I raised myself to my knees, put my hands on the carpet, and faced Amma's soft, strong back. Letting go of my journalist's skepticism, my ego, and my doubts, and entrusting myself to the unknowable, to what is, I pressed my forehead to the floor.

At the time, I didn't recognize the full significance of that moment at the ashram out in Castro Valley. It was only after the many hours I spent with the people who appear in this book, wrestling with their stories, that I came to understand that God's presence isn't located out there somewhere, in something or someone else. It's right here. It's the pilgrim and the pilgrimage. It's the dusty gravel road. The grassy walk to the prayer hall. It's removing the shoes and, like Savitri Hari, baring the feet. It's putting aside the questions and baring the mind, as Cerridwen Fallingstar suggested.

It is embracing my life with joy and gratitude, which I learned from the atheist Anthony Mack. It is noticing that being alive in this moment is the one true miracle and it's been right there in front of me all this time. It is observing life and using my common sense, as Charles Townes and Dwight Dutschke suggested. It is showing up at my little church in the woods from time to time with a mindful of questions, and heading home with even more. It is choosing, along with Geoff Machin, to do the right thing. It is quieting the ego as Martin Verhoeven works so hard to do. It is surrendering to the unknown, to the mystery of who I am and what God is. It is the forehead pressed to the floor at last.

I was struck by no thunderbolts during the writing of this book. Yet slowly, over time, my conversations with the people who tell their stories here convinced me that there is nothing missing from my life, that we live in a miraculous world— that *something is going on.* We can wrestle with that something, but we can't fully know what it is. All we can know for sure is that we are alive and conscious right here, right now, in a world that contains such wonders as frogs, and minnows and polliwogs, and a narrow brown channel flowing into a big blue lake.

It is a miracle that I am sitting here in my writing room in this particular moment, writing these words to you. It's a miracle that you are awake and alive and conscious enough to read them. That's the only truth I've wrestled from God so far. It's all I know for sure. And it's huge.

AFTERWORD: *Creating the Narratives*

Each narrative presented in *Wrestling With God* is the product of a long—and for me deeply rewarding—process that begins with recording an interview with a real person who has generously agreed to share his or her personal story as he or she remembers it.

After that first interview, I send the recording off to be transcribed. When the transcription comes back, I listen to the recording and make any needed corrections in the manuscript. I then proceed to the most challenging part of the process—massaging and rearranging the text into a compelling narrative.

I do my best to stick to the interviewee's original wording, but there are always a lot of ums, you knows, false starts, extra words, and digressions to be eliminated. And, to make the story flow, I typically have to create transition sentences here and there and furnish words for ideas that have been alluded to but not fully expressed.

The next step is to sit down again with the interviewee and read the manuscript aloud together. Corrections are made at this point, more questions asked, and—almost always—more interviews and more readings scheduled. These readings are the best part of the process for my interviewees and for me. We laugh at the funny parts, cry at the sad ones, and feel gratitude for the profoundly meaningful time we have had together.

ACKNOWLEDGMENTS

This book wouldn't exist without the generosity of the women and men whose stories light up these pages. Their spiritual journeys have gripped my imagination and made it impossible for me to let go of them until each had been safely recorded, shaped into a narrative, and published. It's been an honor to work with these inspired storytellers.

My deepest gratitude goes also to the dozens of people whose stories do not appear here, but who spent long hours talking with me and sharing their encounters with God. This book could not have found its way without them. They include: Allan Aistrope, Snjezana Akpinar, William Atherley, Ken Butigan, Olivia Carniglia, Brother Camillus Chavez, Ilene Cummings, Elias Damianakis, Na'ama Firestone, Arife Ellen Hammerle, Mike Hicks, Ernie Hollander, Phil Horner, Tori Isner, Ken Kumasawa, Tom Maley, Carol Lynn Pearson, Hanan Rashid, Jaimee Rungsitiyakorn, Stephanie Salter, Barbara Saunders, Sheldon Winnick, Gary Wirth, and Everett L. Worthington.

The craft of writing is one that takes many years and many mentors to master—if indeed it is ever mastered. As one of my very first mentors, John A. Osmundson at *Look* magazine, pointed out, every writer needs an editor. I've had many. The following wise and helpful souls have taught me much. At *Look*, Patricia Carbine, Irene Fischl, Betty Rollin, and Jack Shepherd. At *Good Housekeeping*, Elizabeth Pope Frank. At *Zodiac News Service,* my husband-to-be Jon Newhall. At the *San Francisco Chronicle*, Joan Heil, Ruth Miller, and Ginger Rothé. At the *Oakland Tribune*, Leroy Aarons, Christine Barnes, Bari Brenner, Kathleen Buckley, Mary Ellen Butler, Robert C. Maynard, Wendy Miller, Eric Newton, Sarah Pollock, Belinda Taylor, and Lisa Wrenn. At the *Contra Costa Times*, Mary Mazzocco, Andrew McGall, and David Risser.

A number of first-rate writing coaches and publishing professionals have kept me company on the road from journalist to storyteller. They include Alice Acheson, Debbie Blue, Sheree Bykofsky, Michael V. Carlisle, Olga Andreyev Carlisle, Charlotte Cook, Carol Edgarian, Jeff Greenwald, Tom Jenks, Moira Johnston, Ann McCutchan, Linda Watanabe McFerrin, Janet Rosen, Mark St. Germain, Jane Anne Staw, and Lauren Winner.

Sustaining me through the long and sometimes discouraging process of putting this book together have been my thoughtful, always tactful, writer friends. Particular thanks to my writing partners, Betsy Blakeslee and Patricia Dove Miller. And many thanks also to the members of my writing groups, Julie Hill Barton, Linnet Harlan, Lisa Howard, and Janet Tezak. Also, Griffin Dix, Kevin Griffin, Suzanne LaFetra, Mike Shaler, and David Stirrat.

Providing inspiration on the journey have been Jean Gregor Gallagher, Judy Greene, Brenda and Mark Richardson, Huston Smith, the women of St. John's Church, and my beloved Education for Ministry companions.

Lending their professional expertise to the project have been editor Brad Bunnin, publicist Karen Campbell, graphic designer

Michelle Lenger, and social media specialist Cheryl McLaughlin. Technical back-up has come from Marcy McGaugh of Writers Rescue, whose good humor and excellent transcribing skills transformed many a free-ranging conversation into a useable starting manuscript.

Special thanks to my agent John Loudon for seeing the potential in *Wrestling With God*. And my deep appreciation to Cathie and Leo Brunnick, Kathleen Mulhern, and Jana Riess for taking on this project and shepherding it through to publication at Patheos Press.

My most heartfelt thanks must go to my family for their willingness to believe in this project simply because I believed in it. That would be my dear children—son and daughter-in-law Peter and Emily Newhall, and daughter (and astute reader) Christina Newhall. And finally, to my loving, ever-patient husband and one-time editor Jon Newhall—thank you, Jon.

CPSIA information can be obtained at www.ICGtesting.com
Printed in the USA
LVOW07s0045090615

441631LV00005B/927/P